AGAINST THE TIDE

AGAINST THE TIDE

Rickover's Leadership Principles and the Rise of the Nuclear Navy

REAR ADM. DAVE OLIVER, USN [RET.]

Naval Institute Press
Annapolis, Maryland

Naval Institute Press
291 Wood Road
Annapolis, MD 21402

Library of Congress Cataloging-in-Publication Data
Oliver, Dave, 1941–
  Against the tide : Rickover's leadership principles and the rise of the
nuclear Navy / Rear Admiral Dave Oliver, USN (Ret.).
    pages cm
  Includes bibliographical references and index.
  ISBN 978-1-61251-797-1 (hardback)—ISBN 978-1-61251-783-4
(ebook) 1. Rickover, Hyman George. 2. Admirals—United States—
Biography. 3. United States. Navy—Officers—Biography. 4. Nuclear
submarines—United States—History—20th century. 5. Nuclear
warships—United States—Safety measures—History. 6. Marine nuclear
reactor plants—United States—Safety measures—History. 7. United
States. Navy—Management. 8. Leadership—United States. I. Title.
  V63.R54O45 2014
  359.0092—dc23
  [B]
                            2014027227

♾ Print editions meet the requirements of ANSI/NISO z39.48-1992
(Permanence of Paper).
Printed in the United States of America.

22 21 20 19 18 17 16 15 14   9 8 7 6 5 4 3 2 1
First printing

This book is dedicated to all the men and women who aspire to leadership and did not have the privilege of personally knowing Adm. Hyman G. Rickover.

It is also dedicated to the woman who reared our two sons by adapting and circumscribing her own professional career—which nevertheless included being licensed by the bars of California, Washington, Idaho, Hawaii, Virginia, and the District of Columbia and becoming the first female chief executive officer of a major company in Japan, first general counsel of the Naval Criminal Investigative Service, associate administrator of the White House Office of Federal Procurement Policy, and deputy and acting director of the Department of Defense Office of Small Business Programs—so I could participate in one of the most exciting periods in the Navy.

Thank you, Linda Bithell Oliver.

Contents

Acknowledgments

As I hope has become evident, Admiral Rickover not only affected how America acted but also how we saw ourselves during a period that much of the world was looking to the United States for leadership. Because of the wide affect the Admiral had I asked a wide spectrum of people to provide their thoughts and comments on this manuscript. Individuals of particular assistance included:

Jim Bailey, Kitty Bean, Jim Blaker, Barry Blechman, Irv Blickstein, Gina Bova, Jay Cohen, Mike Conners, Tom Dugan, Jeff Fowler, Jack Gansler, Paul Gilchrist, Earl Griggs, Mike Hough, Bill Houley, Peter and Rose Mary Hughes, Aaron Johnson, Chris Johnson, Ellie Johnson, David Jones, Bud Kauderer, Jim McAleese, Frank Miller, Vago Muradian, Linda and Tim Oliver, Gina and Michael Pack, Margo Parker, Fred Rainbow, Bob Riley, Ted Rockwell, Steve Spruill, Harlan Ulliman, Mitzi Wertheim, and Leslie Zimring.

I thank each of you.

And with special thanks to Mrs. Eleonore B. Rickover, who is a personal reminder of the admiral's focus on excellence.

1

Why Rickover Is Important

Hyman G. Rickover was the most famous and controversial admiral of his era. He transformed warfare and, in doing so, changed the U.S. Navy, American education, and the defense industry. Rickover conceived and built the world's first nuclear-powered submarine. This gave America a clear technical lead and military superiority at sea over our one peer competitor, the Soviet Union. To make this technical innovation feasible, Rickover cajoled American the public into insisting on better education. This provided him the qualified sailors he needed to staff his ships. Concurrently, he threatened industry as necessary to improve its practices so companies were technically prepared to build safer submarines. Rickover demanded that both academe and industry reach higher than they were comfortable. As might be expected, many in both professions mightily resisted. These conflicts made newspaper headlines.

Within the American Navy, Rickover personally monitored the progress and career of every nuclear-trained officer and demanded continuous improvement of each of them—in fact, his numerous critics were certain he spent his life inappropriately micromanaging the entire submarine force. Even though Rickover's peers loved to hate him, the fruit of his labor was the most powerful naval force the world has ever seen. Before he died, America's underwater fleet controlled each of the seven seas and had irrevocably changed warfare.

No one could have foretold that Rickover would be a success. He did not rise by a conventional path. He was (at best) a late bloomer. During the first two decades of his career, he performed poorly in the very two roles the Navy most values and rewards—command at sea and performance under fire. No matter how rosy the observer's glasses, Rickover was definitely not the warfighter the Navy professed to desire. As a result, during the long years of World War II, Rickover was not assigned within echo distance of the sound of guns.

Nevertheless, by the time he died, Rickover had become one of the very few advanced to four-star admiral rank, and his accomplishments were legendary in naval circles. He was known throughout the world for managing a revolutionary technology from start-up to maturity, altering the culture of a most conservative corporate organization, and shaping the outcome of the Cold War.

Along with his record of extraordinary achievement, Rickover left behind a legacy of knowledge applicable to every organization today. One doesn't need to understand radioactivity to learn lessons from the admiral. Yet, despite his success, few outside the American submarine force use his unique management techniques. Why? Did people hate him so much they could ignore the success of his methods? Do they understand what he accomplished?

Rickover forced a change in the U.S. Navy's culture. In doing so he made many enemies. His adversaries attacked with the viciousness and mindlessness of a pack of stray dogs. Unfortunately, since Rickover chose never to personally answer his critics, false stories continue to be told. Obscuring the truth even more, Rickover wrote no autobiography to set the record straight, and many of his achievements were deeply buried in the vaults of Cold War secrecy.

But the Cold War is now long over, and several of Rickover's peers have contributed to history with biographies, memoirs, or oral reminiscences. At the same time, years have passed. Is a fair evaluation of his methods now even possible, or have the facts become obscured by the swirling of time and the dark of death? To use a boxing analogy, is it even possible to gauge Rickover's tale of the tape?

Yes!

The best measurement involves reactor accidents. This metric is itself sensitive. The world contains adamant supporters of nuclear power as well as diehard opponents. Both camps sometimes even have difficulty speaking to one another in a civil tone. However, I think each would agree that a nuclear submarine provides grand warfighting capabilities for a nation— along with the downside of the danger of a possible reactor accident.

A reactor accident can release large quantities of radioactivity to the environment, killing people and poisoning the earth—this leads to our metric. Only two countries have built large numbers of nuclear ships: the United States and the Soviet Union/Russia. It is possible to list, by nation, the corresponding reactor accidents:[1]

Russian/Soviet Nuclear Reactor Accidents
K-8 (1960, November-class submarine, loss of coolant)
K-19 (1961, Hotel-class submarine, two loss of coolant accidents)
K-11 (1965, November-class submarine, two refueling criticalities)
K-159 (1965, November-class submarine, radioactive discharge)
Lenin (1965, *Lenin*-class icebreaker, loss of coolant)
Lenin (1967, *Lenin*-class icebreaker, loss of coolant)
K-140 (1968, Yankee-class submarine, power excursion)
K-27 (1968, unique reactor in modified November, insufficient cooling)
K-429 (1970, Charlie I–class submarine, uncontrolled start-up)
K-222 (1980, Papa-class submarine, uncontrolled start-up)
K-123 (1982, Alfa-class submarine, loss of coolant)
K-431 (1985, Echo II–class submarine, refueling criticality)
K-192 (1989, Echo II–class submarine, loss of coolant)

U.S. Nuclear Reactor Accidents
None.

This list is history's evaluation of Rickover versus the "peer competitor" he faced and bested. But, like all impersonal metrics, while it may provide important data, it leaves questions unanswered. How did the man become so wise? What were the management methods he used or discovered?

～

This book is not a biography but rather offers a perspective on the admiral's leadership. In effect, I am writing about his management style, not his life. Nevertheless, a short history of the man will assist in placing his challenges in context.[2]

Hyman G. Rickover was born in Poland in January 1900. His Jewish parents fled the pogroms in Europe, immigrated to New York when he was five, and moved two years later to Chicago, where his father worked as a tailor. After having excelled academically in high school, Rickover received an appointment to the U.S. Naval Academy. He graduated in June 1921 in the top quarter of his class. He was assigned to a destroyer for his first duty and then to a battleship. He subsequently attended Columbia

University, where he received an advanced degree in the new science of electrical engineering and, more important, met the beautiful Ruth Masters, the woman he would marry after she had obtained her PhD from the Sorbonne in 1931.

Dr. Masters would have her own quiet career, writing knowledgeably on a myriad of subjects, including her own specialty, international law. Her husband distributed, without attribution, her monographs to all nuclear submarines, where they were avidly read by those of us bored by a constant diet of electrons and decaying nuclear particles. Following his marriage, Rickover converted to his wife's religion of Episcopalianism. They had one son. Ruth died at the age of sixty-nine in 1972. Two years later Rickover married Eleonore A. Bednowicz, another strikingly lovely and accomplished woman who, as a Navy nurse, had cared for him during his first heart attack.

Returning in time to the 1930s, after he had graduated from Columbia, Rickover volunteered for submarine duty (for many years one had to prove oneself on board a surface ship before applying to fly airplanes or serve in submarines).[3] Accepted, Rickover completed the prerequisite six months of submarine training and served on board two submarines. During his underwater career, he and Ruth lived in a picturesque New England town within a few miles of the submarine base in New London, Connecticut.

When he failed to be selected for command of a submarine, Rickover was assigned to another battleship. He then experienced command on board a minesweeper off China, at which time he requested to shift his career designator from "line" (delineating those officers theoretically eligible to serve on and command any ship in the Navy) to "engineering duty only" (the term for an officer who intended to devote his career solely to engineering). In 1938 this career change was approved. Rickover's first engineering duty tour was in the Philippines in the Subic Bay Repair Facility (Cavite Navy Yard).

After a year there, followed by an Asian vacation Ruth documented,[4] the Rickovers reported to the Washington Navy Yard in D.C. in 1939. When World War II burst on the scene, Rickover was head of the Electrical Section at the Bureau of Ships. He remained in this role for most of the conflict. Nearly all accounts laud his performance (but many negatively comment on his professional interpersonal skills).

At the end of the war, Rickover had reached the rank of captain and was within a few years of forced retirement. Several of his classmates, who had themselves commanded ships in the war zone, had already been promoted to admiral. Rickover would undoubtedly have been forcibly retired at the captain rank had he not been selected as one of five naval officers and three civilians the Navy dispatched to Oak Ridge, Tennessee, in 1946. Each of these particularly bright individuals was tasked with becoming technically familiar with what the Manhattan Project discoveries could do for the Navy. Rickover seized this opportunity by the throat and never looked back.

The Navy's plan was to somehow build a nuclear reactor and place it on board a surface ship. However, Rickover recognized the potential of marrying nuclear power with a submarine. He took charge of the small group, maneuvered around obstacles within the Navy and Washington, and gained the personal support of President Harry Truman (and later, President Dwight Eisenhower). In January 1954 the first nuclear-powered submarine in the world, USS *Nautilus* (SSN-571), was commissioned.

Nautilus' capabilities shattered even the most wildly optimistic expectations. After her first at-sea war games, the public began to recognize that the naval battlefield had been profoundly and permanently altered. A few years after *Nautilus* slid down the wooden ways at General Dynamics, nearly a fifth of our Navy's budget was devoted to building thirty nuclear submarines (and operating another sixty), and Rickover had been promoted to the highest admiral rank.

America's nuclear fleet was not built in a vacuum. Our sworn opponent of the era, the Soviet Union, also understood that this new warship was a disruptive warfighting technology. Although the Soviet Union started well behind, soon Soviet shipyards were frantically welding together an even larger number of nuclear-submarine hulls. The race was on!

Rickover was a serious man involved in equally serious business. As he said, "I believe it is the duty of each of us to act as if the fate of the world depended on him. . . . One man by himself cannot do the job. However, one man can make a difference. . . . We must live for the future of the human race, and not for our own comfort or success."[5]

2

Challenges Rickover Faced

Basking in the glory of its role during the sweeping Allied victory in the Pacific, most of the post–World War II U.S. Navy was in no mood to consider, or even listen to, calls for radical change. If the combined navies of Germany and Japan hadn't been able to sink the Allied fleet, where was the need?

The Navy was immense and included myriad rapidly evolving technologies, such as airpower. Military leaders saw no need to adjust to accommodate another new knowledge area. But Rickover believed nuclear technology could not be safely introduced unless naval culture dramatically changed—in itself a Herculean task that would prove to be more difficult than inventing the first reactor *and* the first nuclear submarine.

It is impossible to overstate the massive resistance Rickover encountered when he promoted nuclear power. It did not help that Rickover was not yet a member of the "Admirals Club" (he was far more junior when he began building the first nuclear submarine), was unimposing in appearance (he was short and slight), did not have a magnetic personality (sometimes referring to himself as having the charisma of a chipmunk[1]), and was largely unknown, even in naval circles. Rather than flinching at the difficulties, Rickover publicly engaged with an enthusiasm that often produced news headlines and headaches for the other Navy leaders.

At the time many of us in his own organization shook our heads at the multitude of conflicts in which Rickover personally engaged. Of course, in retrospect, just as his team at the Office of Naval Reactors often noted, Rickover's instincts were usually better than others' careful calculations.[2]

There are good and valid reasons a particular culture takes root in an organization. In military organizations culture assists men and women in adjusting to and accepting danger as well as the emotions that accompany fear. It is difficult to leave the comforts of home and sail for the unknown. It is heartrending to watch friends die and realize there is insufficient time to mourn. It is unnatural for people to kill other people. But this is all part and parcel of life for millions of men and women in the military. Service cultures thus form to help humans cope. Cultures assure individuals that these travails are natural, courageous, and patriotic.

The downside of culture is that it tends to stifle change and reform. A culture is akin to window shades. The lower the shades the less glare from the sun inside and the more comfortable it is for the people working in the room. However, with the shade down, outside events may pass unseen; certainly fewer people inside have the opportunity to recognize that the outside world is changing. As culture becomes stronger, it is equivalent to pulling the shades even lower. Thus, the very tool that helps people aggressively engage in conflict subliminally encourages "a preparation to fight the last war"—the most dangerous path for a military force.

An example of how pernicious this problem can be is the story of repeating rifles, another disruptive military technology. The first of these weapons (Spencer's and Henry's) grew out of the technological marriage of precision manufacturing techniques and new copper cartridges.[3] Both rifles were introduced into the U.S. Army during the Civil War. Unlike previous muzzle-loading guns, the new rifles enabled the soldier to shoot multiple times before pausing to reload. Repeating rifles thus generated a much greater rate of fire than anything heretofore known in history. These transformative weapons were preferentially used by Union forces after 1863, as well as in Europe during the 1870 Franco-Prussian War.

As should have been obvious, against a force armed with repeating rifles it was nearly impossible to overrun a position between successive volleys (while soldiers were reloading). Repeating rifles thus altered an open-terrain charge from a tried-and-true tactic to an invitation to a massacre. Yet, fifty years later, when World War I began, the American Army was still conducting charges on horseback. The downside of culture is that the stronger it becomes the more difficult it is to internally recognize a need to change.

During World War II, the Navy assigned submarines to the rank of a tertiary warship. This was an accurate assessment. Diesel boats were exceptionally fragile; their thin hulls could not withstand even the smallest round from a destroyer gun, and they were vulnerable to air attack. To compound these fighting shortcomings, the vessels were slow when actually submerged. In fact, diesel submarines normally operated on the surface (where their engines had all the air they wanted), diving only to attack or evade. Because of their many weaknesses, during World War II submarines had primarily been used as forward scouts or dispatched to conduct actions against unarmed merchants.

Nevertheless, five years after World War II (while the services were dealing with budgetary downturns intended to free up funding for the postwar American economic recovery), Rickover proposed using vast funds (effectively transferred within the Navy from already impacted aircraft and destroyer accounts) to build his new nuclear-powered submarines. If that were not sufficiently threatening to those who had served in and believed in the value of the (much more numerous) air and surface Navy components, Rickover also wanted to dragoon officer talent from the latter's wardrooms. Given all the cultural barriers he sought to smash, how could Rickover possibly be successful?

The keys were the threat environment, his leadership methods, and his personal work ethic. Even with his exceptional management and personal work habits, Rickover would have failed if history had not also been on his side. It is important to recall the circumstances under which *Nautilus* was born: America was economically recovering from the gold poured into World War II, and there was trouble afoot in the world (the rise of international communism). In addition, the public expected newly discovered nuclear energy to have great benefits for humanity.

Even before World War II was over, the president and Congress had recognized that Soviet Communism was rapidly becoming our new global enemy. As a result of subsequent overt acts and rhetoric (e.g., the Berlin Blockade, 24 June 1948–12 May 1949; the Korean War, 25 June 1950–27 July 1953; and Khrushchev's announcing that the Soviets intended to "bury us"[4]), many Americans believed the Soviets could do exactly as they were threatening. Nearly every American citizen had a tangible dread of the Soviet Union, the vast Red Army, and the stockpile of nuclear weapons the Soviets were building. Aware of the dangers such grim realities imposed, the American public was anxious for an answer—or at least a plan.

At the same time, President Eisenhower was determined to significantly limit military spending and balance the national budget. America was recovering from the great costs of World War II and the Korean War.

Eisenhower thus chose an asymmetric warfare approach to visibly counter the increased Soviet bellicosity. Nuclear submarines had already been approved by Congress. The president placed his high-technology bet on them.

Rickover fueled President Eisenhower's parsimonious predilection by building his first nuclear submarine, USS *Nautilus*, from used parts: a diesel submarine already under construction, liquid-holding tanks from a bankrupt New Jersey dairy, emergency diesel engines salvaged from a minesweeper that had spent the last few years sunk on the bottom of a river, and a refurbished engine room appropriated from a pre–World War II destroyer. He was thus able to build the world's first nuclear-powered submarine for less than $70 million.[5]

Focused as they were on the least expensive method to defend the United States from the Soviet threat, the administration and Congress were predisposed to come down on the nuclear-submarine side of the ledger, and Rickover worked assiduously to keep them on his team. Without their support, Rickover would have had no chance of altering the culture of the Navy—because the latter was not interested in change. With two of the three branches of government on his side, the power of fresh thinking eventually won (at least part of) the day.

In fact, Rickover was not content simply to challenge the 90 percent of the Navy involved in supporting aviation and surface ships. For good reasons he also targeted the functional commands (those organizations and people that don't directly operate ships and aircraft but provide essential support). He started by advocating that his nuclear submarines be built in privately owned shipyards (where he believed the boats would be built to his standards, for he controlled the money) rather than in facilities commanded by Navy admirals (who had myriad ties and thus could certainly resist a captain and even a fellow admiral). It would take many long years before the public shipyards ceased using old processes and procedures.

And, finally, in what was easily the most emotional aspect of the transformation, Rickover made it clear that most of the officers who had previously served in diesel submarines (the same officers who had just popularly "won the war in the Pacific") were not welcome in nuclear submarines.

To understand why this last action aroused so much public interest, one should recall that during World War II, while the rest of the Army, Navy, Marines, and Allies fiercely fought the Germans and Italians in Europe, diesel submarines were directed to the Pacific to hinder, as they might, the encroaching Japanese advance. Carrying out that job was only for the intrepid, and after the first two years of World War II (a period in which the stress of war distinguished the ducks from the drakes in the submarine officer corps), the diesel-submarine force was staffed by an extraordinary group of brave sailors, whose personal boldness more than compensated for their platform's lack of armor and speed. Submariners overcame poorly designed weapons by closing within rock-throwing range to make torpedo attacks from as near as five hundred yards.[6] When they couldn't get close enough while submerged on their batteries, they surfaced to run faster, relying solely on their low silhouette for protection. However, boldness comes with a price tag. Though few, diesel submariners received a disproportionate number of Medals of Honor—seven of the forty-seven awarded the Navy during the war.[7] An equally disproportionate number of submariners died. A higher percentage of diesel submariners were killed in action during World War II than were members of any other U.S. service arm.[8] Given their extraordinary war record, Rickover's reluctance to accept these same officers into the wardrooms of the new nuclear submarines he was building, only a few years after the war had ended, was widely viewed, by the public and the rest of the military, as patently unreasonable.

So, in addition to trying to simultaneously invent and adapt a new technology to an otherwise unvalued naval vessel, Rickover was personally not terribly charming, needed lots of money, had 98 percent of the Navy arrayed against him, was proposing shattering the cookie jars of many other admirals, and was seen as downright disrespectful of the submarine heroes who had just won the first global war. How in the world did he succeed?

3

Planning for Success

More than ambition, more than ability, it is rules that limit contribution; rules are the lowest common denominator of human behavior. They are a substitute for rational thought.[1]

Although Rickover was an extraordinary manager and personally controlled submarine construction for nearly four decades, he was not an able submarine force representative in the Pentagon meetings that dealt with strategy and warfighting. Unlike most senior managers, Rickover accepted his personal limitations for the good of his cause. He would devise a remarkable solution.

Many maintain that a real leader can do it all—can manage anything. They are positive they can. Rickover knew this was incorrect. A real leader needs not only personality but also domain knowledge. Domains are often different. For example, someone who has never flown an airplane should not make rules for pilots. While Rickover became uniquely qualified to build the world's best submarines, he had never commanded one. Even more important, he failed the leadership "sight test." He didn't look like a leader, much less a military one.

Rickover was a slight man, not terribly athletic, and somewhat sensitive about that fact. He also tended to frequently use tools others found offensive. Rickover wasn't terribly interested in polite persuasion. He didn't generally engage unless he believed there was a right and wrong. And why

Note: Unless otherwise indicated, the epigraphs that open the remaining chapters are quoted from Admiral Rickover. Source information is found in the chapter notes.

in the world would anyone decide on the wrong solution? So why should he waste time on this conversation? One of Rickover's favorite guidelines, often imparted immediately before he impatiently (and noisily) hung up the phone, was "Do what is right!"

Rickover also didn't have the persona of a typical submarine warrior. He was an introvert with an unusually high-pitched voice.[2] This was not the picture the public had for the leader of nuclear submarines. They anticipated, as the movies depicted at the time, someone more like John Wayne.[3] Hyman G. Rickover was no John Wayne.

The diesel-submarine officers who exited World War II—the men who had used daring to overcome their platform's clear weaknesses—had a swagger about them. The wakes behind these men were virtually awash in the testosterone elements of the day: poker, booze, women, and cigars.[4] These larger-than-life personalities were acceptable in the Navy because this behavior was popularly linked with legendary submariners. In contrast, Rickover never played poker, did not drink, did not smoke, and avoided any situation that might even imply unfaithfulness to Ruth Masters.

But Rickover well understood the importance of image. He knew his program needed the very best "John Wayne" Americans he could find. Thus, he searched the rolls for men who not only were mentally quick enough to absorb the nuclear-engineering discipline Rickover was developing but could also do what he could not—fill the public image of a submarine officer. He made an unspoken pact with these men. Rickover would teach them engineering and management and stand aside when they took (nonengineering) chances at sea. Wilkinson was his first discovery.

Cdr. Eugene P. "Dennis" Wilkinson was living in San Diego when Rickover drove in from the Borrego Desert one afternoon. Wilkinson was a submariner's submariner. He was smart and brave, was acknowledged as a warrior during World War II, and was not particularly interested in ever concealing his abilities under a barrel. It was already a matter of legend that in 1944 Wilkinson had been on board the submarine USS *Darter* when she torpedoed the Japanese cruiser *Takao* (a warship, not a merchant!). In escaping the counterattack, *Darter* had inadvertently grounded herself on a reef in the Leyte Gulf. The muscular, handsome, six-foot-plus Dennis Wilkinson, USS *Darter*'s engineer officer and strongest swimmer, dived around and under the ship in shark-infested waters, all alone, before determining that salvaging the boat was hopeless. That night Wilkinson successfully ferried a rescue line to a sister submarine. A Japanese destroyer arrived to find an empty submarine an hour after everyone had escaped via Wilkinson's lifeline.

Wilkinson portrayed the event for history in the manner diesel submariners were expected to: "During our patrol in the *Darter* I had a picture of my wife Janice mounted in my stateroom. As we were about to leave the ship, I ran back down, but I didn't get my wife's picture. I got the poker record book—in which I was the one the most ahead."[5]

This was precisely the type of individual Captain Rickover was seeking. I do not know how Rickover learned that Wilkinson was a deadly poker player (gambling was specifically prohibited by Navy regulations, but Wilkinson's pasteboard dexterity was legendary),[6] but it was obvious from his broad chest that Wilkinson was a world-class athlete,[7] and his Silver Star and campaign ribbons were his bravery credentials. Wilkinson was an exceptional leader, and he looked like one.

Unlike others who lead organizations, Rickover did not resent Wilkinson (although Wilkinson and many other subsequent senior officers who gave their all to Rickover were always surprised—and probably hurt—that he did not ever become their friend). Comfortable with himself, Rickover did not require the usual emotional approbation as he went about the business of assessing what was necessary for his program's success. This ability to evaluate a situation without worrying about how the assessment would affect his relationships helped make Rickover unusually effective as a manager.

In 1954 Wilkinson became the first commanding officer of USS *Nautilus*, the first nuclear-powered submarine. Seven years later, when the first nuclear-powered surface ship was commissioned, Wilkinson was assigned as the initial commanding officer of USS *Long Beach* (CGN-9). He would subsequently be placed in charge of the entire submarine force, and in retirement, after the disaster at Three Mile Island in 1979, Wilkinson would, as a civilian, become the president and chief executive officer (CEO) of the Institute of Nuclear Power Operations in order to bring the principles of nuclear navy rigor to the civilian nuclear industry.

Since Rickover wore a civilian suit even after he had been promoted to admiral, Wilkinson was the first uniformed admiral I ever met. Wilkinson came on board USS *Nautilus* at 4:00 one morning in 1969 to present me with the Brass Oak Leaves for my collar insignia the day I was approved for promotion to lieutenant commander. He and I subsequently had the normal occasional professional touches until the late eighties. By then Wilkinson had retired to California, and I was the rear admiral in San Diego in charge of the fast-attack submarines on the West Coast. The Cold War was ongoing, and the Pacific Ocean had recently received the first of a completely new class of submarines, the 688 class, to add to our older 594s and 637s.

In honor of his seventieth birthday, I invited Admiral Wilkinson to go to sea for a few days to experience the new undersea capabilities he had been so instrumental in getting funded. Wilkinson accepted. It was to be a revealing visit.

After the admiral had been "piped aboard," he and I walked through the ship. Dozens of sailors wished to meet the legend. He graciously spoke to each one and listened as they proudly bragged about their new equipment. During the ninety minutes the ship was clearing San Diego Harbor and preparing to dive, we walked the football-field-plus-long ship, passing literally thousands of valves and cables as we did.

Unlike previous classes of submarines, the 688 class, for ease of inspection and cleaning, did not have any covering over the areas in which the ship's runs of pipes and valves and cables were laid. As one consequence, the eight-to-eleven-digit aluminum tags identifying each of the hundreds of electrical cables were visible from the narrow passageways by which sailors moved fore and aft.

Admiral Wilkinson's initial social duties accomplished, the two of us retreated to the wardroom while the ship's crew went about the serious business of getting the ship underwater and properly compensated (submerged and balanced fore and aft, accomplished by taking in or pumping out ballast water until the weight of the ship and the water displaced were the same). The wardroom was relatively small, intended to seat eight to ten officers snugly for meals, but for the moment there were only the two of us.

Admiral Wilkinson settled back on one of the Naugahyde-covered benches, warming his hands with a mug of coffee. He was still a lean man, about six feet two or three, four or five inches taller than the comfortable height in a submarine. As a result, he bent slightly forward at the shoulders. His eyes compensated for this odd posture. They were always focused on his listener.

His first words to me were a challenge: "Would you like to know the numbers on each of the cables in the order we passed them or in reverse?"

For a long moment I thought he was kidding. He was not. He gave me a couple of eleven-digit numbers. I wrote them down and then went out in the passageway and checked. He was absolutely accurate. I knew he was smart; I had not realized he was also a number savant. I decided not to play poker with him. Instead, I pulled out the cribbage board, dealt us each six cards, and asked him how he had begun in nuclear power. The story he told revealed a lot about Rickover's deviously effective determination.

When he first met Rickover, it was 1947. Wilkinson was a lieutenant commander serving as the executive officer on the first missile-firing submarine, USS *Cusk* (SSG-348).[8] World War II was over, and Wilkinson and his wife, Janice, were living in San Diego, where they had both grown up.

Whenever he had free time, Wilkinson would drive up to the University of California–Los Angeles (it was possible to get from San Diego to LA and back in much less than a fortnight in those days) to further his personal study in the mysterious new field of nuclear physics (he had completed everything for his PhD except his dissertation). As he spoke to Rickover at that initial meeting, it became obvious that the captain had screened every naval officer's record before he had driven across country to interview Lieutenant Commander Wilkinson.

Wilkinson told me he had immediately agreed to be a part of the nuclear-power program, and a short time later he and Janice joined Rickover's small team in Oak Ridge, Tennessee, where Wilkinson began work on the design of a core for a submarine reactor.

Rickover was in the habit of taking his own people to meet with experts in the burgeoning nuclear field, and some months after Wilkinson had reported to Oak Ridge, the two of them headed north. Rickover was scheduled to meet Enrico Fermi at the University of Chicago. At that time Fermi was the best-known nuclear physicist in America. He had won the Nobel Prize for Physics in 1938 and on 2 December 1942 had established the first sustainable nuclear chain reaction in the world in the uranium pile he had built on the rackets court under Alonzo Stagg Field, home of the Chicago Maroons football team.

When Rickover and Wilkinson arrived, Fermi was busy with his slide rule, calculating the flux and buckling numbers basic to the new reactor he proposed to build. Rickover and the young Wilkinson sat across from him at his desk. As Rickover and Fermi talked, Wilkinson studied a couple of pages of calculations he could see scattered across the blotter. They were upside down but legible.

After fifteen minutes Wilkinson rose and wordlessly went to one of the chalkboards that surrounded the room. There he began writing from the point he believed Fermi had left safe theoretical ground, through the error he posited in Fermi's calculations to calculations Wilkinson thought led to the correct path. Fermi, who had swiveled in his chair to watch the chalkboard work, stopped speaking to Rickover. He instead pulled his papers over to reinspect his work as he followed Wilkinson's white numbers with increasing interest.

After ten minutes he slowly nodded his agreement. "Maybe."

An hour later Fermi, slide rule in hand, was standing at the board with Wilkinson, saying, "Right," and returning to his desk occasionally to erase some numbers on his papers and scribble in new ones. He was obviously impatient for the Navy men to leave so he could rethink his buckling problem in private. Wilkinson recalled that Rickover was equally ready to conclude the discussion.

As soon as they left Fermi's office, Rickover made a telephone call from a pay phone and then began searching for a Salvation Army second-hand store. When they found one, he purchased a light brown suit, deliberately two sizes too large, for his companion. The following morning it was reveille at dawn for both of them so that they could make the remaining ten-hour drive to downtown Washington. Rickover was impatient. The previous day's telephone call had been to the chairman of the Joint Committee on Atomic Energy, Senator Brien McMahon from Connecticut.

After World War II, Congress had established the Atomic Energy Commission (which would subsequently become the Department of Energy in 1970) as the successor to the Manhattan Project. The Atomic Energy Commission (commonly abbreviated AEC) was fully responsible for the development of atomic energy for the United States. Captain Rickover had already been designated to lead the Navy portion of the AEC nuclear program.

During the Fermi discussion, Rickover had conceived an idea that would prove critically important to the history of nuclear power in the Navy.

Since the AEC was responsible for the development of atomic energy, the commission's budget funded designing and developing the reactors for the Navy's submarines and surface ships. The AEC budget also bought the reactor cores for these ships. The Navy and Department of Defense funded everything else involved in the construction and maintenance of submarines and surface ships.

This arrangement—having two different government agencies or departments in control of two essential pieces of the same program—may seem feasible in theory but is terrible in practice. As the Good Book must somewhere say, having two government agencies in charge of one project was, and ever shall be, an invitation to pass "Go" and proceed directly to hell.

Unfortunately, it was not an easy problem to fix. There was absolutely no chance that either organization would yield any power. Power equals control of dollars, and no one in Washington gives up control of money. Unless one person was in charge (and making the necessary trade-offs and accommodations among capabilities, schedule, and time), there was practically no chance the two parts of the ship would be delivered on the same schedule. This equates to planning for automatic cost overruns.

While Rickover and Wilkinson were speeding across Ohio and Pennsylvania, the AEC was mulling over whom it would appoint to head its naval section. On the one hand, it could be a friend of Rickover's or, more likely, a retired naval officer (who, given the politics of the Navy, would *not* be Rickover's friend). Given the current prominence of Enrico Fermi, it could well be one of the Nobel Prize winner's disciples. If it were the latter, the mantle would probably fall to Dr. Walter H. Zinn, who had recently been assigned the directorship at the Argonne National Laboratory in Illinois, the U.S. center for reactor development. Dr. Zinn was not overly fond of Rickover and definitely not in favor of aggressively pursuing a nuclear submarine until his laboratory had several more years to evaluate the options.

Whoever was assigned, it would still be an invitation to the devil to dance, and Rickover knew that even if he could successfully build and launch USS *Nautilus*, no one, not even the president of the United States, had the power to make two overlapping government agencies work together. It is difficult to manage one agency and impossible to coordinate two. [9] The costs and frustration of a nuclear armada would inevitably skyrocket out of control—and Rickover's vision of a nuclear-submarine fleet would be sunk before it floated.

Vice Admiral Wilkinson told me that they parked on Capitol Hill and walked to McMahon's Senate office. Rickover frequently did not share either strategy or tactics with his subordinates, and this time the only direction Rickover gave Lieutenant Commander Wilkinson was to sit in his oversized brown suit—which must have literally hung on his tall, gaunt frame—on the couch as far away as possible from the senator's desk. Of course, no office in Congress, even for an important committee chairman, is very large, and the chairman and Captain Rickover's conversation was easily overheard.

"Rick," said the senator, shaking his head in disagreement, "I and the members are more than a little inclined toward a civilian appointee. I think that is where we must go."

"Mr. Chairman, I truly respect what you and your committee are doing for our country, but I know that would be a mistake." Rickover paused to let foreboding creep into his voice, and the poker player bones in Wilkinson thoroughly approved of the performance. "And I saw something yesterday that convinced me I should bring this directly to your notice."

Rickover had lowered his voice with the last few words, and Wilkinson watched the senator lean attentively forward. "Mr. Chairman, I have been traveling around the country, and I have assembled the very best team of Americans to work on nuclear power. There is nothing like them in the civilian world."

Rickover inched his heavy chair closer to the senator's desk. "You know I would never say something bad about someone, but that fellow

over there [gesturing dismissively with his thumb back at Wilkinson] and
I were talking to Enrico yesterday in Chicago, and something happened to
make me come straight to see you."

Wilkinson laughed at the memory of that day years ago, took a sip of
his coffee, and spread his large hands out on the wardroom table. He continued his story:

"The senator looked over at me, sized up that ugly oversized brown
suit plus the fact that I was three or four weeks overdue for a haircut, and
his lips came together tighter than a man eating green persimmons.

"Rickover had been watching the senator's face just as I had, and when
he saw the expression he had been expecting, the Old Man closed for the
kill. First, he lowered his voice so that I could just barely hear him, and I
was only six feet away."

"Senator," said the captain, "I have to tell you, that man back there
is the dumbest member of my Navy team, and he is smarter than Enrico
Fermi."

Wilkinson chuckled. "I could see the disbelief spread on the chairman's face."

As Rickover leaned across the desk and used his elbow to inch the
senator's telephone closer to his hand, he consciously pitched his normally
high voice lower. "This is important, Senator. Call Enrico and ask him.
That officer back there's name is Wilkinson. Ask Fermi if Wilkinson is
smarter than him. I am telling you he is."

The chairman looked at Rickover for a second, never glancing at
the young Wilkinson, and then resolutely dialed Fermi. Rickover and
Wilkinson could only hear the senator's side of the conversation.

"Fermi, Rickover is here in my office, and he says that some young
officer named Wilkinson on his team is even smarter than you. I can't
believe that." There was a long pause while the congressman listened to the
Nobel Prize winner renowned for his personal modesty. Finally the chairman cradled the telephone, cast one more doubting look at the tall man in
the brown suit on the sofa, and spoke quietly to Rickover. "Enrico says you
are correct: Wilkinson is smarter than he is."

Even when he was being played, the senator was no one's fool. His
voice contained his suspicion. "What do you propose?"

Rickover pulled from his inside coat pocket the two-page draft joint
committee legislation he had worked on while Wilkinson had driven that
morning. "To maximize the safety of nuclear power in the United States,
I think your committee should establish my Navy team in charge of the
aspects of the Atomic Energy Commission that affect the Navy."

The chairman reached for the papers, slightly shaking his head, his lips again pursed. "I don't see how we could have a Navy team in the Atomic Energy Commission. . . . Perhaps we should just appoint you as the head of that particular portion of the atomic energy team."

Rickover, frowning, let the papers slide from his grasp into the chairman's hand. From his long hours at the poker table, Wilkinson realized his boss's frown was as insincere as the secondhand brown suit he was wearing. "I thought you might have that concern, Mr. Chairman, so I made your suggestion the preferred option."

As our new 688-class submarine finally broke free from surface tension, nosed down, and slowed its rolling, the steward came in to fill our coffee mugs. In another few minutes, many of the ship's officers would arrive, eager to meet Vice Admiral Wilkinson, the first nuclear commanding officer in the U.S. Navy. He would spend each waking moment over the next few days talking to them about his role in building a nuclear navy.

Before the ship's commanding officer, still wearing his brown sweater from the bridge, entered the wardroom, Wilkinson quietly finished his story: "Two weeks later Congress established Rickover as the director of naval nuclear energy in the Atomic Energy Commission, where he has remained until this day.

"No one ever figured out how he did it." Wilkinson grinned, and we both tipped our coffee cups in silent homage to Rickover's foresight and willingness to take risks to achieve his vision.

In this chapter I maintain that Rickover could anticipate the future. I also make the point that Rickover would do whatever was necessary to succeed, including picking individuals very different from him personally but who could better represent nuclear submarines (and his principles) in the rough push and shove of the operational side of the Navy.

Have you ever met anyone who could look far enough ahead to plan for obstacles not yet visible? Is this unusual and extraordinary ability to see the future perhaps one of the discriminating characteristics some unconsciously consider when they seek to differentiate between management and leadership?

In the oral histories of the senior nuclear submariners of the Rickover era, many imply that they never felt close to Admiral Rickover. Recognizing that familiarity is a tool commonly used to bind managers together, why did Rickover not use this device? Is familiarity a useful tool for managers? Was it possible for Rickover, given his own personality? Can a manager be close to his subordinates and still maintain his objectivity?

4

Inadvertent Consequences

The man in charge must concern himself with details.[1]

The first nuclear-powered submarine I served in was *George Washington Carver* (SSBN-656). It was a city-block-long, five-story-high behemoth whose task was to carry (and we hoped never launch) sixteen large nuclear-tipped missiles. *Carver* was one of the forty-one Polaris submarines built during a crash building program of the sixties. The construction boom was intended to restore America's nuclear balance with the Soviet Union.

To get maximum use of the immense capital investment involved in a ballistic submarine and its missiles, there are two crews on missile submarines. I was assigned to *Carver* Gold. The ship had been commissioned (deemed fully ready to go to war) in 1967. Our first ninety-day patrol was in the Mediterranean, and our second was destined for the much colder waters north of Europe in the Barents Sea. We left Rota, Spain, steamed north by northeast around Norway and Murmansk, and settled into our patrol routine.

I remember the area between the Arctic ice pack and the north coast of the Soviet Union as relatively calm that winter. Of course, *relative* is a conditional term. When chilly gales flung long white curls of macramé foam downwind, even several hundred feet down in the deep, our large ship still rolled enough to make strong stomachs queasy.

Safe—at least from any Soviet sensors—*Carver* spent the days steaming long racetrack ovals, interspersed with the occasional lazy eight. In the rear of the control room, black shrouds kept stray light at bay. Inside that curtained area, Lt. Cdr. Bill Johnson and our navigation team pursued a never-ending struggle to update our special inertial navigation system (a finely tuned mechanical device in which three gyros, each mounted perpendicular to the other two, mechanically sensed the movement of the ship). The world had yet to discover the magic of the Global Positioning System.[2]

As usual, all of the officers on board were sleep deprived. Bunks were limited, and qualification standards were high. Consequently, there never was a sufficient number of watch standers. On board *Carver* the officers stood three different supervisory posts: the first responsible for the dive (controlling the depth and trim [upsie-downsies] of our 425-foot-long underwater teeter-totter), the second on the conn (steering, worrying about who in the block-long ship might be thinking about doing something stupid, like opening the wrong valve and letting cold seawater gush in with an earsplitting roar), and the last station, back in the engineering spaces, responsible for maneuvering (managing the reactor and propulsion-plant team).

The Navy had not yet invented equipment that could adequately control the atmosphere inside the submarine, so everyone breathed air containing carbon dioxide, as well as other nasty contaminants, at about thirty times normal levels. We understood that our atmosphere wasn't exactly the same as the one that grew corn and soybeans back in Indiana, although doctors weren't sure of the long-term effects. Without reading the *New England Journal of Medicine*, we could tell excess carbon dioxide affected the bodies' platelets, as our blood took a long time clotting until we had been off the submarine for a couple of weeks. We assumed the air was also the reason for the low-level pounding ache in the back of our brains. Some on *Carver* attributed this throbbing to the Murmansk steam-driven pile drivers. The round-the-clock hammering was evidence of the Soviets' own rushed nuclear-submarine-building program.

Our nuclear-missile package was intended to reduce the city of Moscow to glass. All of us with the proper clearance knew it was a great honor to carry the package. It was America's primary counterattack weapon at the time. In our national war plan, the package was only to be used if the Soviet Union sent its tanks rolling against a European ally (or launched its intercontinental bombers against the United States). The package was the explosive message in the "balance of terror" that President Kennedy had referred to in his 1961 inaugural address.

Being prepared to kill millions of other humans affected all of us on board *Carver*, as it well should. It drove a cold deep into everyone's bones. That may be morally good, but I can assure you it was damned uncomfortable. After several weeks of patrol, even the most intrepid of crew members were more than ready to pass this emotional burden on to the next ballistic-missile submarine crew. Fortuitously, about when the mental weight was becoming clinically depressing to even the least sensitive of us, the next American submarine was already on its way, passing between Iceland and Greenland, headed north by northeast.

However, life is often not completely fair. The very evening we were to be relieved, *Carver* copied an encoded message reporting that our relieving submarine had reversed course and was headed back home. I didn't even need to read the yellow copy as it spooled off the code machine to know this was not good news. Our compatriots had a technical problem that remains classified to this day. But since the event displayed a critical aspect of the admiral's leadership, I need to talk about it. I will thus term the problem *giraffe*, and you can imagine what you wish. It was serious and was the first time this particular problem had ever arisen in the fledgling nuclear-power industry.

When a nuclear problem arose on a Navy ship, the path to a solution was clear. If the ship couldn't figure it out, then Naval Reactors in D.C. was immediately queried. We had copied our sister ship's initial call for assistance. Although it was the middle of night on the East Coast, we knew that Admiral Rickover would soon have his crack staff of hundreds of exceptional engineers working to divine an answer to this difficulty. We could have sat back and waited to read the answer. However, since no one had ever heard of giraffe occurring before and it was possible *Carver* might soon develop the same problem, all of us plunked our butts down around the wardroom table and used this real-life casualty as a training exercise.

We soon determined that, as all had suspected, even though we carried all possible technical information about the ship on board (Rickover was a stickler for all aspects of preparedness), none of the manuals anticipated giraffe. Not only was there no rote answer, apparently no one had even considered the problem might occur. We split into two teams to research, consider, and plan, comparing notes every four hours. What were the options? What were the pros and cons? What would we do? It would be a difficult engineering and management challenge, but after a few hours we believed we had a way forward. In fact, we had not only a primary plan but three options. Our solution was about twelve single-spaced typewritten pages in length.

We all declared ourselves satisfied. I recall I was particularly pleased with my own personal contribution. I was sure I had nailed both the best operational and technical approach. In fact, I was a bit irritated that my fellow officers had not given me the plaudits my nuanced alternative deserved. A few hours later a Morse code message from Naval Reactors in Washington ditted and dotted across the airwaves to our sister ship.[3] It directed one action to ensure the ship's safety. The order was four words long.

All of us immediately recognized its wisdom. Those in the wardroom who had been idly playing cribbage wryly nodded, dumped their coffee cups in the galley sink, and went to bed.

Four words are a bit less than the wisdom contained in our twelve pages.

I carefully reread each line on every one of our single-spaced pages. It was as I feared. None of us had even considered the one safety aspect that could have gotten us all killed. I accepted that I was not as quick as I thought; noted that the engineers at Naval Reactors had truly been on the ball; filed that information away in the back of my brain, right next to my headache; and also turned in for a couple of hours of rack time.

A decade later I spent three months in Washington, D.C., at the Naval Reactors offices. This period in D.C. was scheduled for all senior officers immediately before they received orders to take command of a nuclear ship. The three months were intended to provide Admiral Rickover and his team the opportunity to check on our progress, reexamine our knowledge, and decide whether we were adequately technically prepared for command. Our attendance was required at a certain number of lectures and discussions during these months, but most of each day was spent on individual study.

Time was also set aside to seek out the various Naval Reactors department heads and ask questions. One day I made an appointment to speak to Bill Wegner, Admiral Rickover's longtime deputy for submarines, as I had wanted for several years to pass him and his team a compliment. Once we were sitting in his small office, mugs of hot coffee securely in our hands, I got directly to the point, as I knew he was busy: "Do you remember when [giraffe] occurred—ten years ago up in the Barents Sea?"

"Sure do."

"Well, I want you to know that I was impressed by the engineering response your team provided that day. It was brilliant. I have never forgotten it, and I wanted to tell you so."

Wegner had gray bushy eyebrows. They hid his eyes as he bowed his head down toward his coffee in thought. Finally, he appeared to make up his mind and slowly leaned back in his chair, carefully cradling the coffee to his chest in one hand. "You were impressed, huh?"[4]

"I certainly was. Our ship was also out there on station, and we intercepted the initial trouble report. We brainstormed all night on the problem, but we completely missed the safety issue you guys nailed."

Wegner waved his free hand to cut me off and then circled one finger to indicate the entire building. "So did everyone here."

I shut up in surprise.

Wegner slightly shook his head and paused for a second, apparently ordering past events in his mind. "The Old Man [Rickover] was in an airplane on his way back from somewhere, and we worked up an answer, telling the submarine how they were going to have to operate the plant and the additional procedures to put into place."

I nodded. It was the same approach we had developed that night on board *Carver*.

"It was after his first heart attack, and Admiral Rickover was in the habit of getting some exercise by walking from National Airport back to his apartment," Wegner continued, "so I met him at his apartment door with the draft answer.

"The admiral stood in the hall reading without comment and then invited me inside. He went over to the rolltop desk that was just off the living room, reached into one of the pukas, and took out a half-inch-thick package of yellowed envelopes encased by a rubber band. He fanned through the pile, slipped one out from the pack and handed it to me. 'Tell them this,' he said."

Wegner looked at me expectantly, but I had no idea which way this conversation was headed.

"On the outside of the envelope, in Rickover's handwriting was written 'Giraffe.' After I slit the seal, inside, also in Rickover's distinctive scribble, was a three-by-five card with the four words we sent you."

Wegner continued, "I immediately went back to the office, crossed out the body of our entire draft message, wrote in the four words, and sent it out. The next day I could not contain my curiosity and went in to talk to the admiral.

"It turns out the package of old envelopes were a decade old. In the summer of '58, the idea originated in the White House for Bill Anderson [who later became a congressman from Tennessee and was then the second commanding officer of *Nautilus*] to guide *Nautilus* under the North Pole.

"Rickover couldn't veto the trip because President Eisenhower was personally behind it, but Rick was convinced taking *Nautilus* under the pole was a gamble. The Old Man was worried in part because *Nautilus* was not designed to break through ice. If they could not find a polynya [crack in the ice between glaciers or ice fields], *Nautilus* would not be able to raise a radio antenna to ask for assistance or advice, so he wanted to provide them every bit of help they might need.

"At the same time, Rickover was not interested in anyone else in the Navy knowing how far he was willing to stretch engineering limits in an emergency situation. Rickover believed in operating conservatively and safely. In those envelopes he was going to give up a great deal of his safety cushion to provide an additional operating margin for what he feared was a mistake by the president."[5]

I looked at Wegner. "And these emergency contingency plans remained untouched in the admiral's desk for ten years until the day giraffe happened?"

He nodded. "Yup, after I had handed that one back, the admiral slipped a new rubber band over the deck of envelopes, so as far as I know, they are still there."

Nautilus was actually a prototype—an operating nuclear reactor fitted into a former diesel submarine hull, with the normal prototype Rube Goldberg approach to some applications. However, to gain quick approval for building more nuclear submarines, Admiral Rickover may have implied to Congress and the public that *Nautilus* was a fully capable warship. This was probably 70 percent true. I have had an old, worn component from *Nautilus* sitting on my desk for forty years. It serves to remind me that visionaries often make do with what is at hand when they are in the innovation mode and that selling a new idea sometimes involves imagination.

The famous *Nautilus* trip under the North Pole brings three specific leadership issues to mind. I will speak to the first two now and reserve the third for the next chapter. The first concerns the nature of start-ups. I have never seen a start-up in which people did not become overenthusiastic. As a consequence, those unfamiliar with the details may well believe the start-up is more robust, capable, and survivable than it actually is. The issue for leaders is how to manage that natural naïveté. Rickover did what he could by controlling the quality of personnel assigned to *Nautilus*—the first few wardrooms were all superstars.

The downside of successfully selling a product occurs when an irresistible "buyer," such as the president of the United States, decides he or she needs to use the product immediately—and in a dangerous manner. It is then too late to regret overselling.

President Eisenhower's naval aide, Evan Peter "Pete" Aurand, agreed with Rickover that traveling to the pole, *Nautilus* and her crew were "at [some] risk."[6] Aurand accepted that danger on the basis of what he and the president's press adviser saw as political gain for the president. But Aurand had never been beneath the ice, and he did not intend to be on board *Nautilus*.

This brings up two questions: First, do directors of companies sometimes accept risks they cannot evaluate until the bell tolls? And second, how do leaders avoid fooling themselves about the true condition of their own start-ups?

5

Talent Repercussions

What it takes to do a job will not be learned from a
management course. . . . Human experience shows that people,
not organizations or management systems, get things done.[1]

By the time he was forty, Rickover had made a critical management decision. It was a reluctantly personal one. He had grown to accept that his military peers did not believe he had enough of the intangible "command presence."

He was faced with a dilemma. He would need to find and recruit thousands of people to staff his program. Each would need a deep understanding of nuclear engineering and management. However, they would also have to possess the *élan* to lead sailors into danger. Rickover was an education expert.[2] He believed he well understood what could be taught and what could not. He therefore made a counterintuitive choice. Rather than picking engineers (like himself) and trying to teach charisma, he instead recruited natural leaders who could learn engineering.

He didn't insist on his recruits' becoming technical wizards (although some, like Dennis Wilkinson, clearly were). He looked for potential leaders who were also capable of learning the engineering Rickover believed necessary. He insisted they follow his conservative engineering principles day to day. He wanted to ensure that if, while at sea, they subsequently decided it necessary to take submarines into harm's way, they had the best possible warfighting platform. Action decisions were their choices.

But once Rickover had recruited and trained a group of assertive risk takers, he had the problem of controlling them—for he had staffed his submarines with people who would vie mercilessly with each other to personally count coup against the Soviets. Time would prove that these submariners often went well beyond what Rickover thought prudent.

One of the most extensively documented examples of this challenge involves the second commanding officer of USS *Nautilus*, Cdr. Bill Anderson. The future congressman from Tennessee was a man determined to become even more famous than Dennis Wilkinson, and he had a plan.[3]

America and the White House were not having a good year in 1957. It had started well, with President Eisenhower being sworn in to his second term, but the feel-good atmosphere quickly dissipated as the national unemployment rate approached 20 percent. Then, on 5 September Governor Orval Faubus of Arkansas called out the National Guard to protect those trying to maintain segregation in Little Rock High School. Immediately, the nation was in turmoil. To prevent attacks on black children, Eisenhower was forced to nationalize the Arkansas Guard as well as order troops from the regular Army into Little Rock. Eisenhower, the five-star general, was using his army to protect black children. The public wondered if he and his army had been distracted from the threat of communism.

Exactly a month later, a *New York Times* headline screamed, "Soviet Fires Earth Satellite into Space; It Is Circling the Globe at 18,000 m.p.h.; Sphere Tracked in 4 Crossings over U.S." Below the fold on the front page, a different headline read, "Faubus Compares His Stand to Lee's." Neither headline was good news for Eisenhower. The United States had been trying and had failed to get its rocket program even a few feet off the ground. While the United States was still embroiled in racial tension, the Soviets would launch their first intercontinental missile the following year.

To answer this Soviet technical challenge, President Eisenhower— still focused on recovering from two costly wars—looked for inexpensive answers. Controlling military spending was important to the president's domestic and military priorities. His senior Navy aide was a naval aviator named Pete Aurand, who happened to be a personal friend of the nuclear submariner Cdr. Bill Anderson. Aurand urged the president to undertake a "never-before" crossing under the North Pole with the nuclear submarine Nautilus. Aurand and Anderson would not inform anyone in the Pentagon about the proposed North Pole passage until after the president had committed to the mission.[4] Rickover would be even more of an afterthought.

President Eisenhower and his press secretary, James Hagerty, quickly perceived that this North Pole mission had the potential to swiftly regain technological and military superiority in the public eye. Even more important to Eisenhower, there was no extra cost. The U.S. Navy had already set aside money for a nuclear-submarine building program. Therefore, highlighting a nuclear-submarine success did not have the downside for the president of implicitly endorsing a budget-busting space effort (which the *New York Times* began calling for the day after the *Sputnik* launch) to catch up with the Soviets. For Eisenhower, *Nautilus* was the perfect asymmetric answer to *Sputnik*.[5]

The president knew the political stakes were high. He did not want to experience another "military" failure like the Navy Vanguard rocket program if the mission did not succeed. On the other hand, he desired full credit for any success. Eisenhower accordingly insisted on controlling the timing of any announcements and was clear that the concept and mission were to be treated as top secret.[6]

To drive home this lesson on American technical exceptionalism to the world audience that was avidly watching the communism-versus-capitalism tussles, the president decided to follow the pole trip with news about a submerged voyage around the globe. It would follow Ferdinand Magellan's route and be performed by USS *Triton*, America's first dual-reactor submarine, captained by Eisenhower's previous naval aide, Captain Ned Beach. These two successful demonstrations would showcase Eisenhower's personal investment in this new, and visibly American, technology.

The Magellan trip would finish just in time to be announced at the next summit with Khrushchev and would reinforce the North Pole success.[7] The president directed the Pentagon to plan the Magellan trip as soon as possible. It therefore needed to happen during *Triton*'s shakedown cruise, which was an underway intended to "shake the kinks out" of the new ship, not to demonstrate its abilities on the world stage.

With *Nautilus*' successful passage under the ice cap in the summer of 1958, the first gamble paid off in spades. Accolade headlines appeared around the world. The president held a ceremony in the White House to announce the successful completion of the mission (Admiral Rickover was not invited) and arranged a ticker-tape parade for the whole submarine crew up lower Broadway.[8]

Anderson would later write of the White House ceremony, "I pointedly avoided talking about the strategic military impact of our transit beneath the ice. But it was obvious that *Nautilus*' feat had immediately changed things in that regard." *Time* magazine made the same point, emphasizing how this transit exposed Mother Russia, whose southern borders were protected by satellite states and whose northern shores were protected during most months by miles of pack ice: "In one voyage of one U.S. nuclear submarine . . . the Navy had . . . increased the power of the U.S. deterrent by laying bare the Communist empire's northern shores to the future Polaris-missile-toting nuclear submarines."[9]

Nautilus' crossing under the North Pole was a great achievement for the United States and a brilliant policy move by the president. Although Rickover's expert opinions were ignored and the admiral was kept in the dark about the event,[10] he had the maturity, once the milk had been spilled, to use the crossing to his advantage. He would tout the event to cement congressional support for nuclear submarines. The crossing certainly demonstrated that Rickover had recruited men who could merge boldness with engineering expertise—if only Rickover could stand the daily strain of dealing with such strong personalities.

～

Recruiting the best of the Navy hotshots to work in nuclear power had solved Rickover's need for bold and charismatic leaders in submarines. However, wardrooms of alpha personalities introduced their own unique problems. How was Rickover to guide them? It would be much like herding cats.

Anderson made a new friend in Captain Aurand and subsequently used him to gain direct access to the White House (without telling either the Chief of Naval Operations or Rickover) to propose a mission his ship had not been designed to perform. Anderson well knew that Rickover believed the North Pole trip was technically dangerous and ignored him, as alphas have been known to do.

When the president decided to conduct the mission, Rickover had few options left. By secretly giving Commander Anderson envelopes containing expanded reactor operating limits and other instructions, the admiral attempted to ameliorate the dangerous situation he believed the president and Commander Anderson had established. The president made operational decisions; Rickover could only provide additional technical guidance and latitude.

The North Pole trip was a grand success—for the president, Aurand, Anderson, and nuclear power. Rickover would soon face another situation he could not control. That one did not turn out as well.

6

~

Escaping Responsibility

*Responsibility is a unique concept. . . . You may share it with
others, but your portion is not diminished. You may delegate it,
but it is still with you. . . . If responsibility is rightfully yours,
no evasion, or ignorance or passing the blame can shift
the burden to someone else.*[1]

n the spring of 1963, USS *Thresher*, the first of a new class of nuclear
submarines, sank off the coast of Cape Cod. The ship was lost when an
improperly made piping braze weld separated, permitting seawater to
rush into the ship faster than the high-pressure air system could expel ballast. The day was one of the darkest of the peacetime Navy, with the entire
crew of 129 officers and technical personnel dead on the ocean floor.

It was not the sub's maiden voyage; if it had been, Hyman Rickover
would also have drowned. During the thirty years he was in charge of
nuclear reactors, Rickover made it a practice to be on board the first time
every new nuclear-powered ship went to sea.[2] I suspect he started this practice because he expected the initial at-sea tests of *Nautilus* might experience more than the usual dangers. The *Nautilus*' circumstances were at
least challenging—the first operating reactor was going to sea in a cobbled-
together submarine. Anyone would have good reason to suspect that initial
underway experience might prove a bit iffy.

I believe Rickover continued to ride these initial trials because many of
us needed his presence. Submarines were dangerous business—unnecessarily so. Rickover had not yet successfully won the battle to alter Navy culture. Submarine safety was not paramount in the shipyards and other Navy
staffs. Technology was pushing operations faster than the safety envelope
was expanding. Safety needed to be established as dominant. It couldn't

simply be assumed, for in a shipyard a hundred thousand engineering evolutions occurred each day. Tens of thousands of workers, located in back
shops sprawled out over a shipyard's hundreds of acres, could be working
on equipment that went on board one submarine. There was no chance
that a submarine commanding officer, with a crew of only a hundred,
could monitor every evolution. The shipyard workers themselves had to
absorb the culture of safety.

But the nonnuclear Bureau of Ships was actually headed down a vastly
different path. Indeed, at the time, rather than imposing extra care and
attention, the Bureau of Ships appeared prone to cede submarine technical authority to any iterant shipyard possessing a set of metric wrenches.
This was not a minor problem. Most nuclear-submarine officers believed
the Bureau of Ships' freewheeling delegation was a sure way to get more
submariners killed. In contrast, diesel submariners were comfortable with
this approach.

Nonnuclear engineering duty officers ran not only the Bureau of Ships
but also the shipyards. I suspect every nuclear-trained officer on at least
one occasion witnessed a senior engineering duty officer trying to cover
up a serious mistake. Many of us thought that the *Thresher* investigation
was incomplete at best and that responsibility for the loss (clearly attributable to errors during construction) should have been laid directly at the
Portsmouth Naval Shipyard commander's door. Some held the strong suspicion that the investigation was a whitewash. The Portsmouth admiral responsible for several questionable decisions was the very man the
Engineering Duty Corps had been promoting to relieve Rickover.[3]

If Rickover couldn't control the entire submarine (a nirvana he never
achieved), the nuclear officers whose lives were at risk felt they had to take
action. Many of us became strongly interested in centralizing submarine
technical control so that decisions would be less affected by the immediacies
of waterfront budget and schedule.

Again and again I watched the shipyard engineering duty officers make
decisions that threatened my life in order to maintain their schedule or budget. My life is real. Schedules are paper, and money is fungible. I was more
interested in returning home safely from sea than in meeting any schedule
and budget. Engineering duty officers by definition did not face the dangers
of the deep. For years the other commanding officers and I were often more
attentive to following the technical standards than the engineering duty officers charged to repair our submarines.

But this one issue, no matter how important, does not explain why
Rickover for decades continued going to sea on every new submarine, even
after the shipyards had altered their culture and new submarine designs

were nearly perfected. Since Rickover continued to ride submarines throughout his sixties and seventies and well into his eighties, the rough-and-tumble environment of a submarine at sea was a tremendous physical stress on him. Perhaps equally important, the country was building twelve or more ships a year, and his two-to-four-day attendance at each vessel's trial was a distraction from his other personal and professional responsibilities. Rickover was running one of the largest industrial organizations in the world. He had a wife and child at home. Why did he take the time to put his own life at risk?

I believe it was because he understood that those of us who were sailing his ships needed to see Rickover's personal courage. He understood about leading from the front.

Let me relate one example I witnessed: In 1966 the Newport News shipyard and the submarine's crew had nearly completed eighteen months of backbreaking effort in building USS *George Washington Carver* (SSBN-656), soon to be the United States' newest ballistic-missile submarine. I was assigned to the Gold Crew as the reactor controls officer, and this was my first nuclear-submarine assignment.

The mere act of putting *Carver* out to sea and sailing her across the Atlantic Ocean would target the Soviet Union with significantly more missiles. Our one ship would help redress the missile gap between the two countries. Concurrently, getting *Carver* to sea would be a thumb in the eye to the U.S. Air Force. Among young enlistees and officers, rivalry between the military services is serious business, and the Navy and Air Force were at the time locked in a competition to get intercontinental missiles targeted on the Soviet Union. The new sub would give the Navy admirals a boost toward "correcting," as the admirals perceived it, a strategic (nuclear-missile) imbalance between the Navy and the Air Force.[4]

It is difficult to re-create for the reader the sense of military urgency of the time. America was frightened of the Soviet Union's missile capability. As a candidate in 1960, John F. Kennedy had said there was a missile gap. We believed him and worked accordingly. Our haste produced casualties. On board *Carver* we inadvertently fatally closed the BRA-8 communications buoy hatches on one crew member who had been busy adjusting the limit switches inside the superstructure. We crushed another by lowering the giant Type 11 mast on his chest. Neither fatality slowed progress. We were working sixteen hours a day, seven days a week, at a terrifying pace. We all knew that in our haste to build the ship, we had killed shipmates, and no matter what words were written in the accident investigations, I was there: the deaths resulted solely from human error—and were preventable.

The president of the United States considered nuclear submarines as the front line against encroaching communism. The Congress agreed and was diverting hundreds of millions of dollars from Navy surface ships into submarines. The challenge was exciting, but there was a definite downside. Those involved did the very best that they could. But even though the Navy had thrown human talent at the problem, sometimes the tasks were simply too hard. Some crew members worked until they broke, emotionally and physically. As is often the case in organizations staffed by highly motivated personnel, individuals were too proud to admit they could not keep up. They did not ask for help but took other ways out. Our small crew saw multiple suicide attempts, and some succeeded. My best friend succumbed to the pressure and cut his throat open with a straight razor, in front of his wife. After a year and a half of around-the-clock work, *Carver* was completed eight days early.

Given the haste of building this extraordinarily complicated platform and the errors individuals had observed, some wondered aloud if all the new machinery was going to work properly the first time we went to sea. Were there as many hidden fractures in the ship's thick metal as there were in the crew's psyches? It is not as if the submarine force had the finest safety record in the world.

The loss of *Thresher* was a recent memory. Subsequently, there had been several near calls, especially on board *Seawolf* off the underwater Maine coast.[5] Taking risks and pushing machinery to the limits are the essence of being a submariner. It is important to understand that young military personnel on the front lines of a conflict usually accept risk taking relatively dispassionately—it permeates the career they have chosen. At the same time, no one intends to die, and several nuclear officers instituted more aggressive safety measures. As only one example, Cdr. Dennis Wilkinson, on board *Nautilus*, had begun a process of controlled testing of a submarine before it went to sea.

The testing Wilkinson popularized was essentially a series of cruises alongside the pier after the submarine was built or, as became popular, had been refitted. During the lines-still-tied-up cruise, all equipment was operated and glitches discovered and fixed. Each successive at-sea replication (the hatches were shut as if the ship truly were at sea) was intended to duplicate as best as possible at-sea conditions. Finally, a series of several days was scheduled to test the ship at sea. As I've indicated, Rickover was always invited to attend the first sea tests, or trials.

During these three or four days at sea, we tested the ship at the edges of its operating envelope. This included firing inert weapon shapes at the highest speeds and deepest depths and operating the propulsion plant at its design limits, including full-speed ahead and an emergency reverse. The latter was necessary as reversing power is sometimes useful when a ship is evading torpedoes or when a plastic sonar dome is approaching a concrete pier much too fast.

Before Rickover permitted anyone to declare a ship ready, he wanted to be sure that the ship could operate without restriction at the design limits if the need occurred (for example, if, as later happened to me, some nasty Soviets decided to depth-charge my submarine). And sometimes a crew needed to be pushed to ensure the equipment was tested to its full limits because many military service personnel are normal people with normal fears. Huge noisy machinery rotating at high speeds can frighten more people than ever did my Aunt Ruth with her cast-iron frying pan.

Admiral Rickover had the courage of his convictions—as well as of his engineering. Therefore, on each sea trial, with the admiral sometimes actually seizing the equipment and operating it himself, each crew performed evolutions until they finally got his message that his reactor—just like the diesel engines it was replacing—was designed to serve the simple purpose of moving the ship into and out of combat. If the engineering plant did not so perform, then Rickover modified it. If submariners were reluctant to use the equipment to its full capacity, then that called for a different sort of correction—removal of the men from the submarines—a decision Rickover was also willing to make. In every sea trial, through his personal actions, Rickover taught that the reactor and the propulsion equipment were to be managed, not coddled.

At the same time, sea trials provided the admiral an excellent opportunity to evaluate how well each shipyard was performing (in the 1960s he had nearly a dozen different shipyards on all American coasts simultaneously building submarines). They also provided him early insight into how his own training system was doing in turning out competent officers and enlisted. Personally observing trials was a win-win-win situation for him. But that is not what I best remember.

George Washington Carver had two hatches on its top level. In port they were the access and egress portals. One was in the engineering spaces just forward and to the port side of the maneuvering room, where the watch standers who controlled the reactor, electrical, and steam plants sat. The second hatch was another fifty yards forward, just aft of the conning officer's periscope area. These hatch areas were designed in the event of an underwater emergency to also serve as escape chambers, or trunks.

It is a matter of physics that once a submarine is but a few feet underwater, the sea pressure outside the ship makes it impossible to open any of the submarine's thick steel hatches. One cannot escape the ship until the pressure inside an escape trunk has been raised to match the outside sea pressure (compressed air from the ship's banks is used for this). In a life-threatening event three or four crew members at a time could climb inside the hatch areas and, after the pressure inside was equalized, theoretically escape from the ship and make their way to the surface.[6]

The escape trunk was, of course, unoccupied at sea, and the upper hatch, which opened directly into the sea, was tightly closed. Even the lower hatch, opening into the ship, was normally kept shut. This provided increased protection against an inadvertent mishap. However, to ensure the crew was alerted if water began seeping by the upper hatch (compressed against its metal seat by tons of pressure at the depth we were operating), the drain valve on the escape trunk was cracked open. In this way the conditions in the escape trunk could be remotely monitored.

To return to the 1966 sea trials with Admiral Rickover, we had been at sea three days and were finally down at the deepest depth *Carver* was designed to go. The sea pressure outside the hull was squeezing our huge steel cylinder hard enough to cause the decks to slide several inches inward on their greased athwartship skids (every piece of a ship's equipment is mounted on giant movable frames to accommodate this continuous hull expansion and contraction). Day three of the trial was devoted to testing the torpedo tube handling and firing mechanisms. Today we would spend many long hours at the deepest depth the ship was designed to operate. While there, the sailors in the forward-most compartment would shift huge shapes and weights around in the torpedo room (to ensure all clearances were adequate when the ship's hull was compressed). They would also fire water from the torpedo tubes (a "water slug" in submarine parlance) to make certain the ship's weapon delivery components worked all the way down to the very nadir of the ship's theoretical operating depth.

While the test depth was just within the bottom line of our safe-operating envelope, everyone on board knew, if something went wrong, the chances of surviving decreased exponentially the deeper we were. Being at test depth, especially during a time when submarines were being lost, was emotionally draining. In addition, it was the first time this ship had been to sea. All the submariners on board had been working on dry land for the last two years. Many of the crew members, even those with diesel experience, had never actually been this far below the surface (we were much deeper than a diesel boat could ever safely go). We were well down in the land of giant squid and odd-shaped fish that never saw a hook or experienced a net. Light could not filter down here, and even the whales seldom dived this deep. This far underwater the slightest leak required dramatic action to save the ship. The strain was evident on everyone's face. Whenever someone walked past a sea-pressure gauge—which for the previous two years had rested at zero—the black needle now quivered accusingly at a number reading several hundreds of pounds of pressure per square inch, very nearly up to the red line that marked the maximum safe reading.

The first set of torpedo-room evolutions was expected to require six to eight hours, and maybe as many as twelve. We had been at test depth for about three hours, most of us listening over the sound-powered phones to the torpedomen swearing imaginatively (torpedomen are the Navy poet laureates of profanity). They were using crowbars and sledgehammers to dislodge one particular torpedo skid—the heavy supporting cradle keeping the narrow, long, heavy weapon from bending—that had apparently become pinched during the last two-hundred-foot descent. Suddenly, the upper-level engine room watch stander discovered a stream of water gushing from his escape trunk drain. This was trouble.

The conservative recommendation—that we surface the submarine until we determined the extent of the problem—was immediately relayed to the commanding officer, Capt. Robert D. Donovan. Before he would take such action, Captain Donovan reported the problem to the senior officer on board, Admiral Rickover, who had been reading in the stateroom temporarily allotted him.

Abandoning test depth was not a minor issue. While the problem was real, if *Carver* returned to the surface, we would lose at least a day of trials and possibly several weeks. The torpedo evolutions had to be performed (at test depth) before the final phase of the overhaul could begin. If we returned to port, we would have to fix the escape-trunk problem and immediately return to sea (given the size of the submarine, no chamber in the world was large enough to simulate the stress of test depth on the ship). However, ever since the *Thresher* loss three years earlier, the process of getting a brand new submarine out to sea and down to test depth had become lengthy. Rescue ships had to be scheduled on the surface, specific additional inspections needed to be made, and onetime reports had to be filed.

And our post–sea trial schedule was already tight. We had scheduled events seven days a week until the morning we were to deploy. It was not too difficult to imagine that surfacing to fix the problem in the escape trunk might irreparably delay *Carver*'s initial Mediterranean deployment. Any delay meant our missiles would be late arriving on station to fulfill the U.S. North Atlantic Treaty Organization (NATO) requirement. Other ships would have to remain at sea to cover our tardiness.

We first became aware of an alternative solution when Rickover, who at that time was sixty-six years old, stepped through the hatch into the engine room, a hammer in his belt and a wooden fid in his hand.[7] "Where is the engineer?" he asked.

Lt. Ken Folta poked his early balding head out of maneuvering: "Here, Admiral."

"Call the captain. Get permission to open the lower escape trunk hatch. You and I will lock ourselves inside and fix whatever is wrong."

The admiral pretended as if he didn't even notice Folta's astonished look. "You there," he said, reading my name tag, "Oliver."

"Yes, Sir."

"You will be the telephone link to the commanding officer. You can be the first person to tell him if we die in there."

The words I was thinking were completely inappropriate, but from my mouth came, "Yes, Sir."

The two of them opened the lower hatch, crawled up the steel ladder, and closed and dogged (locked) the lower hatch behind them.[8] I dutifully reported to Captain Donovan events as they occurred.

The rest of the ship waited with apprehension. There followed thirty or forty minutes of muffled banging, with Folta and the admiral stopping occasionally to discuss the best thing to hit next (the correct submarine term for striking something with a hammer is *adjusting*). I relayed all of this as best I could to my very curious commanding officer until the water stopped flowing from the drain and the admiral and Folta backed down the ladder, the latter beaming, both pretty much covered with sea slime.

The admiral handed me the tools without comment. He then proceeded to his stateroom. It was time for him to return to overseeing production of the personal letters intended to be postmarked at sea and mailed immediately upon our arrival back in port to members of Congress and senators who had supported the authorization and construction of USS *George Washington Carver.*

While I watched Rickover's back disappear through the hatch, I realized I had learned a valuable lesson. I was beginning to understand responsibility. I would subsequently put my body between danger and the people who looked to me for leadership.

———⌒———

Rickover was known to hold his subordinates strictly accountable. Other military components often did not share this absolutist view to the same extent. Rickover believed that one strike was often more than sufficient to cause doubt as to an individual's good judgment and that in some cases a person should be removed from the submarine service (and any further association with nuclear power) no matter how expensive the previous training or how many years of previous exemplary service.

Do you agree with Rickover's concept of accountability? He phrased it thusly: "You may share it with others, but your portion is not diminished. You may delegate it, but it is still with you. . . . If responsibility is rightfully yours, no evasion, or ignorance or passing the blame can shift the burden to someone else." Does this definition say anything about current philosophical flirtations with group or team responsibility in the workplace?

In the late 1960s nearly everyone in the submarine force knew someone who had died in one of the two submarine disasters (*Thresher* and *Scorpion*). Only fools were not afraid, but surprisingly few addressed these fears constructively.

Fear of something or someone can be a common problem in the work environment. When it exists, fear causes disproportionate difficulties because so few are willing to acknowledge its existence. We ignore it and thus refuse to think about what we might or should do to ameliorate the reason for the fear. What do people in your organization fear in your workplace?

7

The Danger of Culture

*Good ideas are not adopted automatically. They must be driven
into practice with courageous impatience.*[1]

Going to sea in submarines is a dangerous business. It would be even
more treacherous today had not Admiral Rickover dramatically altered
submarine culture. He made careless deaths unacceptable.

His was a long and difficult struggle. Submariner culture had been
established during the sixty years the United States had operated diesel submarines. These ships were fragile. There was thus a good and noble reason personnel serving in diesel submarines were bred to be bold and accept
risk. Despite or because of the frailness of the underwater warship, diesel
submarines attracted some of the finest young officers of our greatest gen-
eration, and those officers did the best they could to maximize the submarine warfighting capability.

Submariners needed to be especially daring because their ship was so
marginal. However, over time, pushing for performance beyond the limits
of the warfighting platform piles up risk. Over time these piles heap up into
towering and unsteady stacks of dire probabilities. It is impossible to determine how many of the submarine losses during World War II resulted from
the skills of the Japanese seamen and how many should be chalked up to
particular odds against coming home to roost. But culture needs to adjust
when technology changes. Otherwise people die unnecessarily.

Let me give you an example. The personnel operating diesel submarines had learned from experience to always set "Condition Baker" when

coming to periscope depth. Passed throughout the ship, this particular order was the signal for all submariners to cease whatever they were doing and rapidly close the nearest watertight door and the butterfly valves in the huge ventilation lines that carried air between compartments. All on board moved as if their lives depended on it, for history had proved that they did.

The reason for setting Condition Baker was directly related to the physics of sound waves within the top hundred feet of the ocean. Sound waves normally travel in a straight line, which is why you turn your head to the right when someone to your right speaks to you. However, the acoustic conditions in this thin top slice of seawater are much more complex than they are in clean air. This busy aquatic volume often causes acoustic confusion for the submarine. A submarine is safe when she is deep, well below the steel keels of surface ships. It is when she begins her ascent to obtain intelligence or attack that danger arises. Accidents can happen, especially since both parties—the submarine and the surface ship—are often nearly deaf and blind. It would be safer for a submarine to always stay deep. But the engines in diesel submarines demand the air at the surface.

Before deciding to venture up into this near-surface zone, a submerged submarine commonly had spent thirty to forty-five minutes evaluating the situation. The skipper did so with quiet listening, assessment, and experience. Most of us seldom used active sonar in this process. Sonar pings not only were often inaccurate, especially in that near-surface zone, but also disclosed (out to a surprising distance) that a submarine was in the vicinity. When we departed home port on the way to patrol, I always de-energized the active sonar. Accidents didn't happen with the active power fuses in my safe.

During the early years of submarine operation, most maneuvers were conducted in the busy shipping areas off the East Coast of the United States, areas inimical to safe submarine operations. So many submarines were lost to collisions with surface ships that the design of diesel boats was changed. The submarines were constructed so that if one watertight compartment was completely flooded, the submarine would still retain sufficient buoyancy to survive. Along with design changes came procedure adjustments, which returns us to the issue of Condition Baker.

Baker was intended to ensure that only one compartment would flood if a submarine was involved in a collision. I think it was the first evolution I learned when I reported to the diesel submarine USS *Trumpetfish* (SS-425) in 1963. It was certainly one of the three or four submarine procedures taught during every submariner's initial training at the Submarine School in New London, Connecticut.

As might have been expected, when nuclear submarines began sticking their steel noses into the submarine force, Baker was automatically adopted by the former diesel officers who had survived Rickover's screening and transitioned to nuclear ships. Of course, if the operational chain had thought about it more carefully, it would have noted the many differences other than the nuclear reactor between diesel and nuclear submarines. For example, see the following table (values approximate but appropriate):

	Diesel submarine	Nuclear submarine
Time on ocean surface in normal day	90–95%	None
Time near shipping lanes	90–95%	5%
Number of battery charges	One or two daily	One a month

Now why have I introduced into this table the extraordinary disparity in battery charges? Simply because the process of charging batteries, even on board a nuclear submarine, is one of the most dangerous routine evolutions the submarine performs. The procedure produces hydrogen, especially in the last hour of the charge, and hydrogen is not welcome on board a submarine. As most high school chemists have learned, if the hydrogen in a flask reaches the value of 8 percent, it spontaneously combines with the oxygen in the flask. This chemical reaction produces a lot of heat—lots and lots—which on board a submarine is enough to peel the hull back as if it were an overripe banana.

Fortunately, an almost symbiotic relationship existed on diesel submarines between the battery charge and its safety net, the diesel airflow. Although charging the batteries on board diesel submarines was dangerous, no power was available to charge the ship's batteries unless the ship was near the surface and operating its powerful diesel engines. And when the sixteen large pistons in each of those beasts were pounding up and down, each thrust drew so much air through the ship that the evil hydrogen was easily swept away from the battery wells. For example, when I was serving on the diesel submarine USS *Trumpetfish* in the North Atlantic, the submarine charge always resulted in at least a ten-knot cold breeze in the engine room, and we chillingly donned heavy foul-weather bridge jackets inside the normally sweltering space. With that cleansing wind coursing through the ship, hydrogen had little chance of building up on a diesel submarine to the dangerous 8 percent level. Nevertheless, even with this "small" chance for disaster, over the years battery explosions had blown apart seven American diesel submarines.[2]

But, as the table shows, a nuclear submarine operates in a radically different manner from a diesel one. And the extraordinary value of a nuclear reactor was precisely its independence from the need for air. Because a nuclear submarine's prey is warships (as opposed to merchant ships), it tends to hunt well removed from merchant lanes (and consequently far from areas where the relatively shallow water might permit recovery if sunk). Since it doesn't need to surface to charge its batteries and stealth is found below the water, the nuclear submarine normally performs its battery charge deep below.

There was no uncomfortable breeze down at several hundred feet, only the normal hum of the ship's large recirculation fans. In fact, except for some incandescent lamps over the lathe, which would burn brighter at the higher charging voltage, there was no visible indication on board a nuclear submarine when the monthly battery charge was in progress. Safely below, we relied on the ship's atmosphere-control equipment to gradually and safely combine any excess hydrogen with oxygen. By precisely following approved procedures, we could maintain the nasty stuff under 2 percent.

One night at sea in early 1968, on board USS *George Washington Carver* (SSBN-656) (Gold), we were in the last quarter hour of a battery charge. I was on watch in the engineering spaces, monitoring the team responsible for the reactor plant and other engineering evolutions. The hydrogen percentage in the two battery wells was hovering at about a percent and a half, both black needles still well inside the solid green (safe) area painted on the face of the vertical gauge located on the left side of the electrical panel.

Suddenly, a command from officer of the deck rang out over the 1MC:[3] "Set Condition Baker throughout the ship." The ship pitched up, apparently preparatory to proceeding to periscope depth. I could hear heavy steel watertight doors slamming shut throughout the ship. There was either an extraordinary emergency or my teammates in the forward end of the ship had forgotten what the hell we were doing in the engineering plant.

"Stop the charge!" I ordered the electrician sitting in the chair in front of me.

I picked up the 1MC and informed the officer of the deck, "We have a battery charge in progress." I barely omitted "you dumb bastard!"

With the watertight doors shut, no longer was cleansing air scavenging the bubbling hydrogen rapidly being manufactured in every cell in our huge battery. We could only pray the residual air in the battery well would dissipate the hydrogen before it found sufficient oxygen to go about making water babies.

By the time I placed the 1MC back in its cradle, the hydrogen needles had leaped to the red area of the gauge. They were now indicating 3½ and 4 percent. One gauge, two needles, one indicative of the conditions in the forward part of the battery well, the second reading hydrogen concentration in another sector. No one in maneuvering said anything for the next minute except "The charge is off, Sir." Every eye was focused on the climbing hydrogen needles. Everyone was silently willing them to stop. Both quivering indicators had passed 6 percent, and their thin points were creeping ever upward toward the next number.

When we built *Carver*, I had helped install the sensors that fed those needles. An electrician and I had tried to optimally position them in the well, but our efforts had really just relied on a guess. What if I had been wrong by just a few inches—a few tenths of a percent? The announcement of Baker had set in process an evolution that completely isolated the battery well from any cleansing airflow. We were not going to restore the diluting flow until we reached the surface. Were the gauges stabilizing around 7½ percent, or was I engaging in wishful thinking?

Several hours later, having lived, I was eating a grilled cheese sandwich in the wardroom. After an extra bowl of soup, I wrote a succinct letter via the chain of command to the head of the submarine force about why Condition Baker was dangerous for nuclear ships and needed to be promptly eliminated. (We had deep-sixed the use of Baker on board *Carver* before I even sat down to my sandwich.) My letter went not to Admiral Rickover but rather to the Navy engineering staff principally comprising diesel submariners and engineering duty officers. Unfortunately, because these individuals either did not understand or were unwilling to accept how radically different was the new technology, three years later, when I arrived at my next ship, USS *Nautilus* still had the policy of routinely setting Condition Baker while coming to periscope depth. We changed that practice the day I arrived.[4]

Other submariners were not so fortunate. On 5 June 1968, two years after our scare on board USS *Carver*, everyone in USS *Scorpion* (SSN-598) died when that nuclear submarine sank in deep water off the Azores. After a long investigation, no definite cause of the tragedy was found. The inquiry did determine that *Scorpion* appeared to be in the process of coming to periscope depth when an undetermined fatal explosion occurred. Some said that a Soviet submarine must have been at fault (although no Soviet submarines were believed to be in the vicinity, and we tracked their submarines religiously at the time).[5] Others postulated that *Scorpion* must have had a malfunctioning torpedo and been attempting to turn in order to cause the torpedo to shut down. Some considered a battery explosion, but no one was able to imagine the cause.[6]

I always felt that the investigators closed their eyes to the most likely cause because they did not want to acknowledge their own involvement in this tragedy. I had forwarded my letter about Condition Baker via some of the same people responsible for the *Scorpion* investigation.

One of the most vexing challenges of leadership and management is how to induce change in an organization. I often have wondered if our caveman ancestors and their wolf equivalents readily bonded because they both approached change similarly—with trepidation, suspicion, and resistance.

When he accepted the challenge of building the first nuclear submarine, Admiral Rickover realized the engineering accomplishment could not be maintained without major cultural changes in the Navy. A nuclear submarine was going to be a completely different platform than a diesel submarine. To begin with, it would give the U.S. Navy a new capability.

An aircraft carrier or an Aegis cruiser anchored in a foreign port or seen against a skyline sends the message of U.S. resolve and intent. The Navy calls this *presence*. A nuclear submarine lying low in the water and moored to a pier looks relatively benign. Most of the block-long, five-story-high vessel is below water. There are no visible weapons on a submarine. Even a submarine that has more firepower inside than the rest of the American fleet still does not cry "presence."

What a nuclear submarine does have is the ability to go anywhere in the world there is water; no matter how hostile the conditions, it will survive, observe, and kill. The Navy developed a term for this. They called it *deterrence*.

Rickover was fond of pointing out that a nuclear submarine became a viable deterrent the minute it left the pier and slipped below the surface of the sea—and getting under way required only a reliable engineering plant. Of course, no warrior would conceive of not having an operational weapon system, but his point was still valid. The nuclear submarine did not need airplanes flying, radars pulsating, and guns firing (all these capabilities had been adapted—with indifferent results—to diesel submarines during World War II). The nuclear submarine simply needed to be able to get to sea and submerge. Once it was below the water, it was the most feared deterrent in the U.S. arsenal. Therefore, the United States needed personnel in the nuclear-submarine force who could master the nuclear technology and were willing to work the hours necessary to keep the complex engineering plant reliable.

For four decades Rickover interviewed each nuclear candidate to ensure the individual was motivated to make this sacrifice (or, for those from a diesel submarine, which typically did not require such effort, to make the adjustment). Rickover was biased toward recruiting an individual without submarine experience rather than accepting someone who had spent years working with an obsolete technology. Rickover believed that just as a foreign language was easier to absorb in one's youth, it was more feasible to learn good work habits the first time and as a younger officer. Given the choice—which he fought to get and keep—Rickover frequently bypassed sea-experienced diesel submariners in favor of surface officers with no submarine experience or graduating college seniors.

As you might expect, the very premise of "not being good enough" for nuclear submarines was incomprehensible for those diesel submariners already wearing the gold dolphin insignia on their chests. They strongly resented the prestige downgrade involved in leaving submarines. The loss of extra danger pay paid to submariners (but not those in surface ships) was also not inconsiderable. To magnify the problem, the former submariners were not welcomed with open arms in their new homes, for, naturally, the surface community resented the increased competition these sailors brought for the limited number of promotions and the plum job assignments.

This situation produced continued discomfort in the Navy, as well as the submarine force. On one night I remember well, after a late-evening "discussion" among a group of nuclear-trained and diesel officers at the Officers Club in San Diego, several diesel officers returned with chain saws and reduced the club to sawdust and shorter timbers. Cooler heads prevailed the next day, and rather than conducting a military investigation that would accomplish nothing, over the next couple of weekends, these same diesel and nuclear officers rebuilt the wooden structure to its former ambiance.

Even though it was wrenching and painful to personal and professional relationships, the elimination of the diesel culture was a necessary and farsighted tactic in Rickover's overall strategy to remake the Navy. I first served at sea on board a diesel submarine and twenty years later commanded the last squadron of diesel submarines remaining in the Navy. It is unpopular to say, but remains nevertheless true, that a diesel submarine is a much less complex platform to maintain. A diesel submarine demanded boldness but much, much less work to keep operating. In addition, a less-capable diesel submarine provides the citizens of the United States significantly less security than a nuclear submarine does.

The old guard didn't want to hear this, but I was uniquely positioned to know it to be so. I am convinced that despite the unrelenting personal attacks on him, without Rickover insisting upon dramatic change, many more of us would have died while building the nuclear-submarine force.[7] As Rickover commented in testifying about the *Thresher* disaster, "Our problem is in the submarine staffs where nearly all of the people are non-nuclear people, some of whom have a deep resentment against the nuclear navy because it has put them out of business."[8]

Reading through the biographies, reflections, and oral histories of naval leaders contemporaneous with Rickover, one finds that this major conflict is veiled by the personal friendships and bonhomie that existed among many admirals. However, this disquiet was real. It was fueled by many things but fanned by the other admirals' almost universal distaste for Admiral Rickover, a coolness that, given his prickly personality, he reciprocated.[9]

I was troubled at the time by the openly expressed harsh emotions. I thought that if only we could all sit down together, these problems could be solved. However, in retrospect I do not know how the cultural change could have progressed differently. A change in deeply rooted beliefs can never be accomplished by reading thoughtful white papers. People don't resist change for rational reasons—they resist emotionally. Successful managers of change develop a competing passion. They provide both a new vision and an arousing reason to change. I have seen cultural changes that worked, and I have seen failures. Once you have established the rationale, the best way to make change happen is through a cult of personality. The submarine technology transition needed the personality cult Hyman G. Rickover provided.

The nuclear platform, armed with extraordinary weapons (both conventional and nuclear), depended less on daring rogues than on people who could master the technology and who were willing to work the hours necessary to make it reliable. These people were part and parcel of the submarine platform transition from a warfighting afterthought to the backbone of our Navy. The importance of the submariners' role in the transition made it necessary for Rickover to look for the right people to establish a new culture in the submarine force.

When implementing changes, a leader should consider several questions about culture, including the following:

- Is it possible to establish a new culture upon the bones of an older one? Are there limitations to this approach?
- Have you ever seen major change achieved? How was it done—through memos or the establishment of a personality cult? How long did the culture transition take to carry out? Did the change stick or revert?

8

Future Shadows

*Free discussion requires an atmosphere unembarrassed by any
suggestion of authority or even respect. If a subordinate agrees
with his superior he is a useless part of the organization.*[1]

A s a consequence of the Cold War tension between the United States
and the Soviet Union, as soon as USS *Nautilus* began racing circles
around every other warship in the oceans, every American shipyard,
including several of marginal capability, was tasked to build submarines. Even with this Herculean effort, the numbers of U.S. submarines never
matched the size of the Soviet submarine fleet. However, America would
always retain a clear margin of quality over the Soviets—a lead Rickover
and his successors would inexorably widen.

This advantage was a consequence not merely of superior engineering
and sensor design but also of the tactical ability of the American submarine
officers. Their talent and learned skills were linked to the outcome of the
Cold War. When the Soviet Union finally collapsed and more information
escaped the iron curtain, it became apparent that those skills were in great
measure dependent on a critical decision Rickover had made almost half a
century earlier.

This leads to a story: It is common knowledge—and true—that nuclear
power produces invisible, invasive, and deadly radiation. It is also generally
accepted—but false—that nuclear reactors are synonymous with bombs.
The average American knows radiation comes from atomic bombs—like
the two America dropped to end World War II—but few citizens have
the time or inclination to learn much more about nuclear physics. As a

consequence, no matter how sophisticated they might be about the world around them, many Americans never overcome the misapprehension that a nuclear reactor is some sort of mini atomic bomb.

Consequently, it was historical serendipity that nuclear submarines were ever built in the United States. Yes, the concept had politically powerful supporters, Rickover was a driven individual, and the technology was there to be exploited. But the perceived overwhelming threat was the crucial reason nuclear submarines came to the Western Hemisphere. America was more frightened of the Soviet Union than anything else, including invisible radiation. Rickover understood this approval caveat.

He (nearly alone) could also envision a future when the fear of the Soviet Union would subside. When that day came, radiation from submarine power plants would still be present—and then would be a concern. Rickover organized for the future. The admiral not only recognized what the citizens should demand long before the public found its voice; he also accepted responsibility for those demands. Since he felt personally responsible, he ensured that all the men and women working for him also willingly accepted this challenge. Rickover realized that to address this problem in part, he needed to become a trusted voice and face to the public. Even though he was inherently shy,[2] Rickover knew it was important to the nuclear program for him to maintain a special condition of confidence with the American people. Rickover knew that his credibility with the public—trust that flowed from the housewives, the men on the cereal production lines, and the secretaries in the offices—was absolutely essential if the Navy was going to be permitted to build this new force that would so impact the outcome of the Cold War. Rubbing shoulders with the people in the White House and Congress was not nearly sufficient.

The public didn't actually know what we were doing with the submarines. Nevertheless, Rickover needed its support for the funds to keep building these revolutionary platforms. He also needed the public's acquiescence to keep nuclear ships based in American cities (if the submariners had to live in remote areas, recruitment would become immeasurably more difficult, as would maintenance and repair of the ships). In addition, Rickover needed citizens to keep sending their sons to serve on board nuclear ships. If Americans ever became more frightened of the possible downsides of nuclear power than they were of the Soviet Union, Rickover believed they would not listen to any argument, no matter how factual or well phrased. (And, of course, Rickover was correct, for the public essentially curtailed the American commercial nuclear electrical power program after the Three Mile Island accident, regardless of the logical arguments supporters of nuclear energy made.)

Rickover also knew there was an important ancillary axiom to this confidence. The public would trust him only as long as no one who worked for him made a serious error. His public integrity depended on all of us in his program. This meant his veracity was dependent on whether two thousand to three thousand personnel could remain responsible seven days a week, twenty-four hours a day. How fragile! It was a wonder Rickover could sleep at night.

As part of his implicit deal with the American people, Rickover ensured their sons and daughters would not be hurt by the radiation from his reactors. To that end, he specified that American submarines would be designed so that a sailor on board would receive less exposure than an American farmer. Not only did Rickover accomplish this, but the design radiation levels he set as safe on his first submarines have proved, more than a half century later, to be just as harmless as he intended.

Of course, to establish those numbers, he had to fight his own staff on four issues. First, designing the reactor shielding to limit radiation as Rickover desired required more engineering ingenuity and inevitably additional weight and volume within the submarine devoted to shielding. Since, after the sensor equipment trade-offs, a larger hull was necessary, the shielding resulted in a slower submarine for the same size power plant. Second, the United States was in an arms race for survival. We were taking many risks. Rickover's own staff and other experts asked, Why not accept the radiation levels everyone else considers safe? Soviet nuclear submarines could steam faster than ours with the shielding, giving them improved survivability through speed. Third, as Rickover's critics correctly postulated, we who served in the nuclear program (since we were young and patriotic) were more than willing to expose ourselves to much higher levels of radiation than later proved to be safe. And, fourth, as is nearly always true with new technologies, there was no real "authority" on safe radiation levels, and those individuals who did have an opinion nearly unanimously believed in a higher level than did Rickover.

Admiral Rickover made his own decision. He made it against the advice of his staff. He made it against the advice of all the other radiation "experts" in the world. He made it on the basis of his imperfect knowledge of the issues but also from his instinctive understanding of engineering and people. It was his personal decision, and it would prove decisive in our race against the Soviet Union.

Why? Because we would, over time, learn about the cumulative detrimental effect of radiation on the human body. I am a good example. I performed my initial training on the first submarine prototype reactor built in the recently designated National Reactor Test Station. It was a site in the middle of the Idaho desert, sixty miles from the nearest town, approximately equidistant from the small farming communities of Blackfoot, Idaho Falls, and Pocatello. Not only did I spend six months of hot days and freezing nights getting my hands dirty learning how to make the reactor and all its equipment work together; I several times entered the high-radiation areas in the world's first reactor compartment.

Because of my time in Idaho with the original S1W reactor,[3] as well as my subsequent duty on board *Nautilus*, and because I sometimes did things less brilliantly than I should have, I had much more exposure to deleterious radiation than most. However, because of the limits Rickover set at the beginning of the program, I still received less radiation exposure during my thirty-year career than would an individual working an equivalent time in the Rayburn House Office Building in Washington, D.C. (where workers encounter a surprisingly high exposure from the low-level uranium [pitchblende] contamination in the granite used in construction) or a ski enthusiast who lives in Aspen (the higher one goes, the less the atmosphere protects against radiation produced by the sun's solar flares).

How and why did Rickover make this decision? When Rickover set the radiation standards, he somehow anticipated what people might learn over the next few decades about the dangers of ionizing radiation. The admiral did more than worry about the immediate correct answer. He also projected how the technology would likely develop. Essentially, he was thinking decades ahead even while the alligators of daily life were nipping at his ankles.

Before he designed the first submarine, Admiral Rickover had gone around the world talking to the men and women currently working with radiation. Among others he visited Enrico Fermi in Chicago and the successors to Marie and Pierre Curie in Paris. He asked each to recommend a "safe dosage" for human exposure. Rickover listened and took notes. He then divided their suggested number by the factor of a hundred.

He was adamant that his engineers design to his lower number (the first nuclear submarine, USS *Nautilus*, had a few locations where the radiation level was slightly above his desired levels). Despite a great deal of pressure from many engineers and authorities who wanted faster submarines, Rickover insisted on his lesser limit for succeeding submarine designs. A decade later, when it became obvious that we could operationally manage within the radiation limits he had previously set, he lowered the guidelines by another factor of ten, telling us only that we had no innate understanding of the long-term effects of something new that we could not see, taste, or smell.

Across the ocean Soviet engineers adopted submarine designs that permitted much higher levels of radiation in the occupied spaces. Their boats moved at higher speeds, which worried us (and we would consequently build faster torpedoes to compensate). However, with that additional speed came a disaster for the Red Navy.

The tactical danger was that higher levels of exposure resulted in human radiation sickness. As the Soviets began long patrols far from their shores, their predicament became so acute that stories began leaking out of that closed society that submariners were undergoing enforced rest periods on the shores of the Black Sea. We first thought these vacations were a status perk for the highly prestigious submarine corps. It was only much later that intelligence disclosed the enforced leave, away from nuclear plants, was to permit the sailors' bone marrow to regencrate.

Several years later we realized that strategically, the impact on the Soviet submarine force skill set was even more pronounced. For example, I was assigned to a nuclear submarine for sixteen of my first twenty years of service. I was normally on board the ship every day when we were in port, and nuclear submarines not in shipyards were at sea for an average of more than three hundred days a year. As a consequence of all my time at sea, if only through osmosis, I learned a great deal professionally. Soviet submarine officers with precisely my talents, forced by their health to spend half of their useful careers on the beaches of the Black Sea, impatiently waiting for their red and white corpuscles to stabilize, could never be my professional equals at sea—no matter how many warfighting manuals they read or how many exercises they war-gamed on a tabletop or computer. It was not until the Cold War came to its abrupt end, and we began to uncover the many technical errors the Soviet navy had suffered, that we fully realized the strategic disaster Rickover's foresight had avoided.

However, for Rickover's prudence to have an effect, he also had to have in place programs, processes, and procedures that actualized this prescience. For decades, several of those processes centered on a "film badge." Everyone likely to be exposed to radiation wore some form of this detector above his or her waist. The badge was one method (of several, all equally stringently enforced) used to ensure we all remained within the prescribed ionizing radiation exposure limits. In the case of the badge, which relied on the visible reaction of picture film to gamma and neutron radiation to monitor levels of exposure, once a month the hospital corpsman assigned to the crew would replace the individually numbered badges, develop and "read" the old film, and update individual exposure records.

As is often true with new measuring techniques, the process of developing, drying, and evaluating the films was exacting and involved several opportunities for error. Therefore, the precise measurement and documentation of film-badge exposure was always a special point of focus. The film badge was—as Admiral Rickover emphasized each time he spoke to a group of nuclear officers—a key component in demonstrating to the American people that we were serious about controlling human radiation exposure.

Those of us on nuclear submarines accorded the film-badge process the respect Admiral Rickover demanded. While I was executive officer on board USS *Haddo* (SSN-604), I spent hours in the cramped spaces of the ship's darkroom (which also served as the submarine sick bay when film developing was not in progress) supervising our medical corpsman. I wanted to ensure he was following the process exactly as written. Additionally, once a month after his periodic report was completed, instead of spending an evening with my family, I would lock myself in the darkroom and randomly reread and rescore 5 to 10 percent of the previous month's films.

During the first two years I was on board in the late 1970s, *Haddo* was having her reactor fuel replaced and other maintenance work done. It shouldn't have taken as long as it did, but the shipyard owners were busy shifting their work into the more profitable business of surface-ship construction. As a first step they had transferred their best talent from managing nuclear submarine overhauls to the facility on the other side of the river. The new shipyard on the other bank would build surface ships, beginning with the DD-963 Spruances. The shipyard had won a lucrative contract. These ships were powered by gas turbines, not nuclear reactors. Therefore, the West Bank shipyard managers would have only to answer to the (much less demanding) nonnuclear section of the Bureau of Ships, and not to Admiral Rickover.

On our side of the river, in the suddenly talent-poor East Bank submarine overhaul facility largely abandoned, we experienced expensive delays attributable to management incompetence. Not only were millions of taxpayer dollars wasted; our ship was more than a year over schedule to get back to sea and reengaged in the conflict with the Soviet Union. All of us on board *Haddo* were anxious to depart this disaster.

Finally, the work on our submarine ended, and a team from Admiral Rickover's staff in Washington, D.C., flew down to certify that our crew was competent to start up and operate our new reactor. The process involved oral and written examinations, as well as "observed evolutions."[4] Everything appeared to go well.[5] But the standard inspection had one new wrinkle. When the team arrived, an inspector handed our corpsman several previously exposed "test films" and told him to develop them, read them, and report the results. The corpsman promptly trundled off to his little room to whip up a new batch of developing fluid.

At the end of the two-day examination, we were informed we had failed. I remember the occasion as if it were yesterday: the Naval Reactors' senior inspector held up a piece of paper with three columns, the first two typed and the last handwritten. Eight-digit film numbers were in the left-hand column, three-digit exposure values (the expected answers) were in the second column, and the third contained handwritten values replicating those our corpsman had provided. It was clear that our results were more than 25 percent low, which was much too inaccurate. The inspector folded the paper once and handed it to me. Failed. We were now officially in the lower 10 percent of the submarines of the fleet. To recover we would have to spend sixty days training to prepare for a complete reexamination of all facets of our performance. They would not be fun days. Equally depressing, we would have to remain another two months with the shipyard management that had already stolen an extra year of our lives. Our commanding officer gave me a look of disappointment. Neither of us had expected this. He had already planned to take a two-week family vacation in Michigan, and he decided to proceed while I worked on a recovery plan.

After the rest of the officers had gone home that night, I lingered on board the ship with my thoughts. It was a warm evening, as all are on the Gulf Coast. Once the sun was safely well below the horizon, I went topside to walk. The waterfront was relatively peaceful. The only lights apart from those at each ship's gangway were the occasional colored spray of a cutting torch parting the shadows. The only sound was the slap of water against the creosote pilings under my feet.

Could we have made such a gross mistake? No one had actually been in the tiny darkroom watching the corpsman develop and read the check film the inspectors had provided, but I had trained our corpsman for two years. I knew he was more than competent. The answer had to be *no*.

What were the other variables? There were only two: the company that made the check film and the organization that exposed it. I watched the flickering gas flares from the gulf oil drill rigs for an hour or two while I smoked a couple of cigarettes.

The next morning I stopped by my spouse's bank and made a withdrawal. Once on board ship I sought volunteers and provided two crew members with cash from the raid on our children's college fund. One volunteer was to remain in uniform. He was to proceed to Bethesda Naval Hospital. Bethesda historically provided medical care for the president of the United States as well as members of Congress and those Navy personnel stationed or living in the vicinity. Bethesda was also the closest military hospital to the Naval Reactors' offices, was commanded and run by a doctor with the rank of admiral, and possessed gamma and neutron sources (which the hospital normally used for medical procedures).

I knew Admiral Rickover was proud of squeezing every penny in his programs. He would never approve paying for his own radiation sources but would always be in favor of getting them for free. His staff would reflect those values. The inspection team had said this check-film procedure was a new part of the inspection. The Bethesda hospital would be the closest place to D.C. to expose film. I wondered if all Rickover's staff shared his attention to detail. Did the Bethesda staff?

The second individual changed into civilian clothes and caught a bus north for Rochester, New York.

Within a week both sailors were safely back on board *Haddo*. Our two volunteers had great careers ahead of them as undercover operators. The one who had gone to Bethesda had obtained as much information as we needed within forty-eight hours. It seems the individual at Bethesda Naval Hospital charged with exposing the Naval Reactors' film had not quite understood that radiation decreases much faster than one might suspect as the distance from the source increases (inverse square law). He had thus computed the film exposure incorrectly and furnished Naval Reactors with the wrong data (in other words, the individual was inexpensive and worth every penny). This was great news for the home team and explained the number discrepancy, but the information from New York was even more interesting.

Our man in Rochester had gained employment by Kodak as part of their night cleaning crew and, simply by wandering around, talking to employees, and perhaps bumping against a file cabinet or two that had inadvertently popped ajar, had determined that Kodak had produced a bad batch of film several months earlier. Rather than properly destroying the film, Kodak had instead negligently shipped the batch to the Navy and requested payment. Our man in Rochester had even obtained the film file numbers. Naval Reactors' check-film samples had indeed been performed using that bad batch.

Since the commanding officer was out of town, I composed and sent what I considered an appropriate message to Admiral Rickover. It detailed what we had found in only a week. I asked that our ship's examination grade be changed to satisfactory and that his team apologize to our crew.

Within a few hours we received notification we were going to be reinspected the next day. I was livid. We weren't the problem. Naval Reactors was the organization that had screwed up. I had expected Rickover to acknowledge the mistake. Instead, he was now demanding that we go through all the trauma of a reinspection. The notification message provided the specific time the inspector (the head of the section responsible for radiation safety) would arrive. It also specified that I was to personally pick up the Naval Reactors' representative at the airport and provide him transportation.

It is difficult to accurately describe my state of anger when I met the chief inspector at the airport the next afternoon. The Naval Reactors' representative was carrying only a briefcase when he stepped off the airplane, and he imperiously raised his hand to me, palm out, like a school crossing guard, when I started to speak, "Wait."

We walked to my car in silence, exited the parking area, and pulled onto Highway 10, at which point he gestured toward the best restaurant in this small town. He had his door open and was out of the car before we completely stopped in the parking lot. By the time I reached our table, a waitress had already taken his gin and tonic order. His briefcase lay on the bench. He was sitting very upright, hands folded in front of him.

I slid into the bench opposite, more than ready to now join battle. His right hand rose, palm again toward me. It didn't look like he had a long lifeline, and I was ready to help confirm that. He blew his nose into a handkerchief, folded it, and thrust it back into the side pocket of his suit. Only then did he rather hurriedly speak, as if he were trying to avoid letting me get a word in: "Your reinspection consists of me flying down here, buying you dinner, and signing a sheet of paper in my briefcase which says the USS *Haddo* is satisfactory."

He took a breath. "I then pay for your dinner out of my own pocket, hand the inspection report to you, and make it back on the last plane out tonight to D.C. I need to be at my desk tomorrow morning at eight o'clock when I am to provide Admiral Rickover a much longer report on the details of how I managed to screw all of this up."

The waitress brought his drink, and he took a long initial sip while simultaneously holding up his index finger from the unoccupied hand, indicating he could use another right away. I ordered an "unsweetened" iced tea (since this was Mississippi, the modifier was a necessary part of the order) along with catfish.

At dinner I discovered he was actually a pretty interesting fellow. And of course his boss was also. For it did not matter how correct I was about a particular issue, Rickover was not about to cede an inch of control as to who in the Navy decided whether a particular nuclear ship was satisfactory or unsatisfactory. At the same time, the admiral did not even wince at what others would consider my outrageous behavior:

- sending a sailor into the plant of a private contractor to uncover evidence of possible malfeasance,

- deploying a spy into the most prestigious government hospital in the Navy medical establishment in order to look for incompetence, and
- essentially accusing the admiral's personal staff of ineptitude and demanding an apology.

As long as one was correct, Rickover only judged results.

A few months later, after USS *Haddo* had passed through the Panama Canal and was riding at her new berth at Ballast Point, the *San Diego Union* carried a short article in the business section reporting that Kodak had paid the Navy a large fine for shipping a bad batch of film.

⌒

Rickover demanded accountability—of himself and of the individuals he placed in responsible positions. In the companies and organizations with which you are familiar, do the people in charge strive to be personally accountable for the most dangerous parts of their business, or do they seek to distance themselves from risk? Why do many organizations accept practices that do not demand accountability? Does yours?

9

Knowing You, Knowing Me

I don't mean to suggest by that that he is a man who is without
controversy. He speaks his mind. . . . But the greatness of the
American military service . . . is symbolized in this ceremony today,
because this man, who is controversial, this man, who comes up with
unorthodox ideas, did not become submerged by the bureaucracy,
because once genius is submerged by bureaucracy, a nation
is doomed to mediocrity.

President Richard Nixon[1]

Some years ago Tom Waits had a best-selling song in which he recalled the emotional rollercoaster he experienced in telephoning a former girl-friend: "Operator, number, please: it's been so many years—Will she remember my old voice . . . ?"[2] Navy commanding officers certainly never had any difficulty identifying the unique high-pitched voice of the Father of the Nuclear Navy. They had a good idea when he might call. Rickover was as regular as the swallows returning to Capistrano. If a prob-lem of consequence had occurred on board your ship, you prepared your-self. When his red pencil arrived at your name, Rickover was going to dial your number. He was going to demand that you personally justify your actions. If you could not do so to his satisfaction, the admiral—in a time-honored Navy tradition—might very well tell you to hit the road on your way out of "his" nuclear-power program.

I was twenty-eight the first time seventy-year-old Admiral Rickover called me. It was 1970. I was serving as the officer responsible for the engi-neering plant on board USS *Nautilus*, the celebrated platform Rickover had been personally responsible for conceiving. While *Nautilus* was truly remarkable when compared with a diesel boat, she was inferior to every other U.S. nuclear submarine ever built (with the possible exception of USS

Seawolf, which that day was moored to the other side of the same pier in New London). *Nautilus* and *Seawolf* were the first and second nuclear submarines in the world and had been used hard in their early years. Some of their makeup was running, and there were ladders in their stockings. Nevertheless, they were both still expected to be front and center whenever the hostess tinkled her silver party bell. Getting old is a bitch.

The day I received my own first telephone call from Rickover, I had been in the reactor compartment repairing a problem (which still remains classified and unique, so while it was a different breed of "giraffe," we'll reuse that label). While my men and I tried to fix the situation, the commanding officer decided he should let someone know we had a problem. He selected the president as that someone.[3] I am sure that President Nixon was interested in what the officer had to say, but he turned out not to be an expert in giraffes. Therefore, when my boss hung up, President Nixon made the wise choice of calling the man he would soon promote to four stars. I was not privy to his conversation with Admiral Rickover.

I do have some understanding about what happened shortly after Nixon and Rickover spoke. For example, I am told that Admiral Rickover immediately telephoned my commanding officer and gently pointed out that when there was a difficulty on board one of his submarines, he did not enjoy first learning about it from the president of the United States. He quizzed my commanding officer. He apparently did not receive an explanation with which he was completely satisfied.

Back in the reactor compartment, we were busy. We had made one unsuccessful run at the problem and were developing a second plan when the commanding officer stuck his head through the access three stories above: "Dave, telephone call."

"Captain, I'm really busy."

"Admiral Rickover wants to talk to you on the wardroom telephone." (This was years before big bulky portable phones and decades before mobiles.)

"I'm *really* busy." It seemed to me that my job was to solve giraffe and the captain's role was to talk to Admiral Rickover.

"He *really* wants to talk to *you*!"

Okay, that was clear.

I climbed the ladder and quickly dealt with the precautions necessary when working with radioactivity. I then followed the captain to the wardroom, taking the receiver he handed me. "Yes, Sir."

A familiar high-pitched voice wasted no time in pleasantries: "What is going on?"

"I screwed up."

"I know you are screwed up. How *much* are you screwed up?" (To be completely accurate, these were not the precise words Rickover used. The admiral had a proclivity for more graphic speech.)

In fifty or so quick words, I explained giraffe.

"Do you need any help?" His voice was calm, not accusatory. As soon as he realized I actually knew what had gone wrong and was taking full responsibility, his attitude turned immediately to helpful.

In point of fact, I had no idea whether I needed help, but at the same time I was not terribly interested in "advice" from any of the non-nuclear-trained staff then available in New London. I only knew I wanted to get back in the reactor compartment before I inadvertently spread radioactive contamination. "No," I answered.

"Do you want anything at all?" Again, his voice was unruffled.

I stopped shifting from foot to foot and thought for a second. "I could use some more pure water" (to provide a backup supply if a different event unexpectedly occurred).

A second later the world was back to normal. I was listening to a dial tone. It took us eight hours to solve the immediate problem.

Three days of frantic work later, all giraffe consequences had been dealt with, we had written an explanatory report to Admiral Rickover, started up the reactor, and gotten under way to maintain our scheduled Mediterranean deployment. It was just after midnight when we backed away from the pier. The Thames River was quiet. All the personnel who worked the river and lifted the bridges were in bars with beers or home with families. As we left the submarine base, we partially submerged to slip the top of *Nautilus*' sail a few inches under the railroad overpass that blocked our egress to Long Island Sound. We would be far at sea by the time day broke.

After we had cleared Montauk Light, the commanding officer went below, leaving me alone on the bridge with my thoughts and the undulating sounds of the sea. It was only then that I reflected and realized that in one of the largest submarine ports in the world, after the president of the United States had been notified of a unique problem on board the submarine most intimately connected to Admiral Rickover's reputation, even while the problem dragged on for the entire working day, not one individual had stepped foot on our pier to check on an officer (me) not yet in his thirties. That is, except for the rear admiral personally driving the water truck, who had asked the topside watch to please inform Lieutenant Oliver that fifty thousand gallons of pure demineralized water was available on the pier if he needed it.

Many years later, when I knew Rickover better, I still questioned, as I know readers do, how he could have so entrusted such a callow youth (and even the commanding officer, who was only ten years older). The answer did not lie in the particular abilities of the individuals, but rather in the management system Rickover had created within the larger Navy. The admiral had in effect discovered a Rosetta stone of management. He had, through ten to fifteen years of study, trial, and error, determined how to instill W. Edwards Deming's process control in submarine engineering and training without simultaneously constraining operational boldness.[4]

Key to his trust was that long before the day Admiral Rickover first called me on the telephone, he knew me well. He had personally interviewed me for nearly an hour, as he did every new officer applicant, before I graduated from college. He had subsequently received weekly or quarterly reports on my progress during the initial six years of my personal development. In addition, before he had entrusted me with the care of the *Nautilus'* engineering plant, I had returned to his headquarters in Washington, D.C., to undergo three days of tests. The tests were extensive: an eight-hour written examination followed by four hours of orals. In addition, to receive the *Nautilus* assignment, there followed another full day of give-and-take with the admiral's deputy, Bill Wegner.[5] In short, none of his several thousand officers were blank pieces of paper to Rickover, and those he intended for particularly difficult duties (which *Nautilus* certainly was), he selected very carefully.

On the subject of nuclear power, Rickover knew from the beginning it was important to scrutinize safety. He believed this could be accomplished only through carefully monitoring the people he admitted as well as their training. He did not delegate that responsibility because the sad truth is that most leaders, even those in nuclear power, lack the backbone to truly manage people. Management does not just involve praise—anyone can do that, although many do not. Management also involves looking someone in the eyes and delivering the hard message that the employee has reached too high.

What Rickover understood better than anyone I have met is that people are much happier when they are busy working on something they can accomplish. An individual finds this much more satisfying than completing a human resources performance improvement plan that will only qualify him or her to once again fail at a job for which he or she is unsuited.

He also understood that fellow workers do not appreciate having a nonperformer in their midst. It does not matter whether the person fails because he or she is not trying hard enough or is insufficiently talented. If the worker can't perform, the team suffers. Failing to remove a nonperformer delivers the denigrating message that the manager does not value the group's work.

The personal interview process that Rickover conducted was essential to the culture he was instilling and demanding within the nuclear program. This new culture demanded changes that would prove difficult for his public critics to understand. Nearly everyone in the Navy bridled over Rickover's selection process for nuclear power for several reasons, including the following:

- the rest of the Navy didn't use such a process;[6]
- the powerful Bureau of Personnel didn't control the process (so they fought it tooth and nail until finally there were sufficient nuclear-trained officers within the bureau to quiet the old guard critics);
- industry didn't use such a process (that is, have new recruits interviewed by the CEO), so there were no commercial paradigms to point to as justification;
- people with apparently good résumés were rejected;
- sons of important men were not selected;
- people with good political connections were not selected; and
- Rickover never explained the process or his decisions.

Rickover had to deal with an unusually large number of personalities loosely described by pop psychology as Type A. However accurate the label, how do you reward risk takers who often resist guidance yet have the leadership characteristics necessary for the future success of the organization?

Rickover cursed "like a sailor" as the saying goes. He could even embarrass other seafaring souls. His cursing frightened some so much they froze and couldn't adequately explain themselves, and it caused others to unnecessarily back down, rather than hold their ground. It produced an environment not conducive to the free flow of information. Was cursing Rickover's great flaw? Are great men born with a flaw, or do men with power let their flaws creep up on them, like Carl Sandburg's fog, on little cat feet?

10

Wooing and Winning

*It is a human inclination to hope things will work out,
despite evidence or doubt to the contrary. A successful manager
must resist this temptation.*[1]

As mentioned in the previous chapter, Admiral Rickover personally met all volunteers (or those who had been gently coerced into applying) for submarine duty at least twice if they made submarines a career and three times if they were screened to command a nuclear ship. The "Rickover interview" was a contentious topic at the time—and still generates arguments—but it also conveys great lessons about successfully managing people.

The most press and public angst was directed at the initial interview. This interview was an absolute prerequisite for the six months of intense class work Rickover required of all nuclear submariners. Before the advent of nuclear submarines, the Navy had permitted incoming ensigns to select the area of the service in which they would like to serve. The person with the highest class standing, both at the Naval Academy and in the Reserve Officer Training Corps, would select first from the available jobs, the second highest would choose second, and so on, until all job opportunities were filled. Rickover altered the rules of the game. Although the class valedictorian might choose submarines, Rickover reserved the right to independently decide if an applicant had the right stuff to even train for his nuclear-power team. Once an applicant was selected, he or she entered training intended to bestow the equivalent theoretical knowledge of a master's degree in nuclear engineering, and this training was immediately followed by six months of practical experience on an operating reactor. Thus, the formal nuclear training regime required twelve months and was expensive. Rickover did not want someone likely to fail taking up a precious seat, even if that predicted failure was not an academic one but instead an inability to adapt to all the pressures of a submarine.

So, to the rest of the Navy, the nuclear-propulsion interview process involved change. Intentionally or not, the interview conveyed the notion that Admiral Rickover and perhaps other nuclear submariners considered themselves superior to officers in the other Navy components. The first of these impressions was not terribly positive, and the second was seen by many as impertinent. To add insult to injury, as the superiority of nuclear submarines to other warships became evident, some submariners began to refer to the rest of the Navy simply as "targets."

Let us review why applicants considered the Rickover interview process so unpleasant. First, no one, no matter how mature, actually likes uncertainty. It was not that any of these particular young men (there were no women in submarines until 2010[2]) were in great need of a job. In general, Rickover restricted applicants to young officers who had already proved themselves at sea and to college graduates in the top 10 percent of their college classes (Phi Beta Kappa at one of the schools Rickover believed to be a top engineering school). All of these particular men had been pursued since they were in high school. Not one was worried about where he was going to find his next dollar. In fact, nearly every college student Rickover interviewed was facing only one question: Would he graduate cum, magna cum, or summa cum laude? Consequently, nearly all expected excellence and deferential treatment. That was not quite Rickover's style.

About 80 percent of the interview process proceeded as the interviewee might expect. The candidates came to Washington, D.C., and made their way to a ramshackle World War II–era wooden building (later torn down in the renovation that resulted in the reflecting pool and grassy areas near the Washington Monument). There, on the second floor, the interviewee would go through three lengthy discussions with staff members about the interviewee's academic and personal life. The young hopeful then waited (sometimes several hours) until Admiral Rickover was available.

There are many stories of interviews with the admiral. Most focus on the fact that Rickover did not treat the interviewee in the manner the applicant would have preferred.[3] In almost every case the admiral had already read the individual's academic record and was prone to pounce on any deterioration in grades from one semester or year to the next or any grade less than an A. Not surprisingly, Rickover did not accept discovery of true love, excessive use of alcohol, or ownership of a new car as acceptable justifications. If the interviewee offered what the admiral believed were lame excuses or blamed others for his failures, the admiral reportedly blasphemed—with the young man still in the room. He often abruptly told applicants to leave his office. Some he gave a second chance. Others he simply did not.[4]

No matter how few or many failed the Rickover interview (his staff recalls 10 percent failures—participants remember a higher number), those not accepted, along with their parents, sponsors, and schools, frequently believed the interview process to be "unfair." The young men now adjudged lacking had never been turned down for anything in their short lives—nor had been treated so cavalierly. Sometimes, in their disappointment, the rejected men or their sponsors related their stories to anyone who would listen. It was as Senator Russell Long of Louisiana said about tax reform: "Don't tax me. Don't tax thee. Tax that man behind the tree!" In this case, they railed, the man behind the tree must be Admiral Rickover.

Perhaps they embellished their experiences. I do not know. I was not present for any interview but my own. Rickover gave a rationale for the confrontational approach of his interviews, but I believe his explanation was constructed for the press (when he was under heavy attack for his style of interviews) rather than truly representative of why he conducted the interviews as he did. Rickover said at the time, "They all have excellent résumés. . . . So what I'm trying to find out is how they will behave under pressure. Will they lie, or bluff, or panic, or wilt? Or will they continue to function with some modicum of competence and integrity?"[5]

As I have previously noted, Rickover was pushing to alter a great deal of Navy culture. Cultural change involves broken glass. It was much easier to curse Rickover for his tough interviews than it was to damn him for changes that were improving safety. As a result, his interviews became such a public cause célèbre that the admiral soon adopted the practice of having a third person in the room to maintain a record of what was actually said.

I believe that these interviews were essential to the success of the nuclear program and that Rickover was actually working a much more important goal than ascertaining how easily a young man was rattled. Rickover often worked from gut instinct. He had worked with thousands of young officers. I think he was looking to weed out those bright young men who would, a few years down the road, inevitably crack under pressure.

Those rejected might never understand that not being chosen was the best thing that could have happened to them (because they could immediately move on to a career for which they were better suited). But they were human beings; they had been rejected, and their feelings were hurt. I can understand the young men's angst; however, I was always surprised by the number of outside critics, ignorant of the unusual demands of the program, who felt they could be so shrilly derisive of Rickover's judgment.

I do know that later in my life, after I had run several businesses, I was even more impressed with the value and uniqueness of Rickover's approach. Frankly, it is an exceedingly rare organization that believes a twenty-year-old merits any of the CEO's time—no matter how small the organization or brilliant the applicant. The company human resources system is designed to put these young men and women in a learning role so they will be worth an hour at some future time. In the commercial world I spent that much time interviewing applicants for vice president positions. These applicants could potentially make a difference in the bottom line, which was the object of business. I could not afford to make an error.

If the corporate world CEO does not spend an hour with new recruits, then why did Admiral Rickover? It wasn't because he had time on his hands. He was immensely busy—going to sea with each new submarine, visiting members of Congress, personally calling nearly two hundred commanding officers on the telephone every few months, visiting shipyards and factories. Yet he made available the hundreds of hours necessary to talk to each new applicant. In 1962 alone, when the nuclear-submarine shipbuilding program was in a frenzy of activity (thirty submarines were under construction that year), Rickover decided that he had run out of an adequate number of acceptable candidates for nuclear power. He sought and obtained special permission to select six hundred officers from the existing surface force (that is, nonvolunteers).[6] These men alone represented fifty days of extra interview work for him that year, assuming twelve-hour workdays.

Why Rickover insisted on these interviews was a piece of his professional puzzle that I could never quite make fit. I wondered for years. It may well have been his concern about safety because goodness knows that every officer was personally responsible for some aspect of reactor safety. Then one day a senior officer who would eventually become a four-star admiral (the very peak of the Navy profession) inadvertently demonstrated to me another aspect of the wisdom of Rickover's insistence on personal interviews.

This particular future admiral, whom we will call Jay (precisely because that is definitely not his name), called me late one afternoon. His submarine was being decommissioned and the crew dispersed to other ships. We were both serving as executive officers (the second senior officer on board our respective ships), and he called as a courtesy to let me know he was sending us one of his "better officers," a young man whom we will call George. The conversation went something like this:

"George is really a good person. You will like him. He has a beautiful wife and three lovely children."

"That's great, Jay. We are soon deploying [sailing to the Western Pacific for thirteen months], so it will be good to have another qualified officer on board to share the work."

There was a short silence from Jay (a prescient quiet to which I should have been more attentive). "He is not yet qualified, Dave. I was just ready to certify him, but we got caught up in taking the [reactor] core out, and," he chuckled, "you know how it is."

"I understand," I foolishly replied. "If you say he is a good officer, we will get his qualifications finished right away and get him on the watch bill."

"He is a good man," Jay heartily continued. "You have my word." Ah, the exquisite use of language—for I would subsequently find out George may have been good man, but he definitely was not a good nuclear officer. Jay was a master.

It was true that George had a lovely blond wife and three wonderful towheaded children. He was a nice person and pleasant at our frequent wardroom parties. He also was sincere as hell. But he could not keep up with either the daily work challenges or his peers. Like a lame dray horse, he dragged his fellow officers down to his own stumbling pace.

After a year and a half of everyone trying to help him—a period in which George did not perform useful work, broke practically everything he touched, and proved an immense burden to all the other officers—I finally transferred him out of submarines. The Navy assigned him to manage a small base on a nearly deserted island, a job I understand he did quite well.

With one fewer set of hands after George had left, more work got done and morale improved. In the quiet of my room one night, as I was thinking about this increased productivity and berating myself for waiting eighteen months to pull the trigger on an obvious conclusion, I finally realized an aspect of what Rickover was trying to accomplish with his initial interviews. Rickover knew that nearly every supervisor finds it difficult to tell someone that he or she is not "right" for a particular team. This weeding process is relatively easy when picking an athletic team, for while everyone hates not making the squad, God-given hand-eye coordination is fairly easy to gauge. But when the real need is for superior mental speed, agility, and logic, all of which have been allotted by that same God, how many managers are truly comfortable in making the assessment?

In nuclear submarines each officer must rapidly process large quantities of information under a great deal of pressure. Mistakes involve tangible penalties, which may include your shipmate's life. Because a submarine has a relatively tiny crew with only about a dozen officers in the wardroom, there are a limited number of people to do officer tasks. One individual's inability to perform adds a heavy stone to the backbreaking load every other officer is carrying.

Nevertheless, nearly every manager I ever met would do almost anything to avoid telling a stumbling subordinate he or she was not quick enough to do the job. I believe Rickover, in his initial interview process, was conducting an early screening to compensate for the human weakness he knew all his subordinates brought to work each day.[7]

Jay, the officer who called me about transferring his wardroom member, was not strong enough to tell George that he was not suitable for nuclear submarines. Instead, he passed George on to me, effectively wasting another two years of George's life, as well as making success more difficult for me and the team of officers on board my ship. Jay had done no one any favors.

In fact, most managers are very like Jay. Few sufficiently understand what is best for the organization and the absolute necessity to cull and reassign those who are not mentally or emotionally fit for the role. Most managers fail to prune even when it is obvious subordinates are physically making themselves ill in trying to perform (one secret to management is to understand that nearly all try their utmost—there are few slackers). Most leaders talk about "their most critical asset" as if staff members were a herd of cows grazing on an open range back amid the hills. Rickover actually managed people.

*

People normally try to perform to the best of their ability. Those who continually fall short will keep trying, and failing, until answers as cruel as suicide appear rational. What is the supervisor's role? Is reassignment harsher than the methods individuals will ultimately adopt to keep their sanity? Which is affected more by the failure to reassign nonperforming personnel: the big organization or the lone individual?

At one point, in a time of great stress during the Cold War, responsibility for which was disproportionately felt by the nuclear-submarine force, we were short on nuclear sailors (so there was constant pressure to fit square pegs in round holes). The number of suicides in the Pacific submarine force soon reached hundreds of percent in excess of the national average. We finally adopted the motto "There is no shame in sending a young man home where he can learn another trade; but sending him home in a box means he had an uncaring manager." Within a few months our suicide rate dropped below the age-adjusted national average.

Do most supervisors manage personnel well? Are failures caused by manager deficiencies or by human resources system limitations?

11

~

Innovation and Process

One must create the ability in this staff to generate clear forceful
arguments for opposing viewpoints as well as for their own.
Open discussions and disagreements must be encouraged.[1]

When Rickover and his acolytes finally achieved control of the submarine force in the early 1970s, nuclear submarines began to be managed differently. Rickover was open about the concepts he practiced in the nuclear reactors program. He was also extremely vocal and public in critiquing the errors he observed in the traditional Navy techniques. The distinctions he drew produced tension within the Navy. Rickover welcomed it. He was convinced good management was a serious subject and open disagreement was the way to reach a decision.

Rickover and the submariners he had trained also believed the stakes were nothing less than the lives of the men who went to sea in nuclear submarines. Real-world events underscored his view. Public and preventable losses included the 1963 sinking of the nuclear submarine *Thresher* with all hands, and this was followed by the complete loss of *Scorpion* and her crew in 1968 and the near sinking of *Seawolf* a few months later.

Yet the larger Navy strongly resisted the changes Rickover advocated. Most of the Navy officers as well as the presidentially appointed civilians in the Defense Department believed Rickover's approach both unnecessary and too costly. In fact, those who sailed on surface ships even accused Rickover of espousing the adoption of bad management practices.

Both sides were sincere but working from two completely different premises. When surface-ship engines stop, the ships merely slow down until someone is available to come on board to fix them or until a tow can be arranged. Submarines spend their lives far from possible assistance. When their motors stop working, submarines slide inexorably deeper until the pressure crushes the hull or they surface to face destruction or capture. These basic facts of physics and environment understandably lead to different priorities. As with the proverbial chicken and pig attending a charity ham and egg breakfast, one is mildly interested in the outcome, while the other is involved.

As both the Vietnam and Cold Wars were ongoing at the time, all in the Navy had a lot on their individual plates. The air and surface communities were fighting a completely different war than were submariners (who bore the brunt of the work in countering the Soviets but were only peripherally involved in Vietnam[2]). Nonsubmariners were not spending much time worrying about the smallest Navy organization—especially one so little involved in the Vietnam War. However, since submariners' valid concerns were continually ignored, we came to a conclusion (that was maybe not logical intellectually but emotionally felt consistent at the time). We decided the non-nuclear-trained officers in the Bureau of Ships were either (1) trying to kill all the submariners or (2) simply stupid. Neither answer contributed much toward good fellowship within the larger corps of officers.

At the same time, under the strain of the war in Southeast Asia, ignorant of what submarines were accomplishing in the Cold War, the larger Navy began to resent the submarine force (submarine officers made up less than 5 percent of the officer corps but commanded nearly a quarter of the Navy's warships). This professional disagreement quickly turned personal in the Vietnam War years. Most of the Navy was convinced the nuclear submariners were

1. Deliberately destroying the diesel-boat culture (and thus unfairly increasing the competition for command in surface ships),
2. Receiving more than a fair share of the money devoted to ship and aircraft construction,
3. Individually receiving more pay than their peers (submariners received the same danger pay as aviators, but it was evident to all who read the daily papers that the aviators were earning their money in Vietnam),
4. Acting like prima donnas too good to be more than peripherally involved in Vietnam, and
5. Being promoted faster and to higher positions and receiving a disproportionate and undeserved number of prestigious awards.

Of these, points 1 through 3, as well as 5, were accurate (promotion often follows from having a command, but of course, I would dispute "undeserved"). As for the prima donna issue, no submariner was permitted to hint, even to his spouse, about the top-secret work keeping him out of Vietnam.[3] The kindest words used by some in the Navy in belittling the men in the nuclear submarines were "robots and functionaries." Those critics on the sidelines who desired to appear more balanced, but who were equally ignorant, tended to refer to nuclear submariners as "unimaginative" and "process bound."

In the midst of this personal acrimony, sailors on both sides had overlooked that—driven by the crushing workload on board each nuclear submarine, the high operating tempo (submarine time away from home port was much more extreme than that for any other community), and Rickover's rigid insistence on safety—the nuclear force had been forced to develop a method of simultaneously accommodating innovation and process. The nuclear force had adopted a policy of ruthlessly discriminating between operations that should be treated as ordinary and other work. If the work to be done was judged routine, then it was completed in accordance with precise procedures. These rigid procedures were written to require only a moderate level of talent, training, and supervision to achieve the proper degree of safety. By this careful differentiation between tasks, submarine leadership attention could be redirected and prioritized to those nonroutine management functions that required special attention, intellect, or innovation.

Even with the limited number of truly superior individuals in the pool, Admiral Rickover had recruited—by using this deliberate division of labor—senior managers subliminally encouraged to work on the most challenging problem sets, while the much larger group of officers and enlisted focused on following established processes. As a result, the submarine force not only thrived over the years but, more important, continually improved. Throughout Rickover's life and beyond, each day the nuclear submarine became safer and more effective. Continual improvement eventually became the hallmark of the submarine force.[4]

However, strict procedures, training, and processes were neither popular nor generally accepted by the rest of the Navy. Having two such different approaches in the same organization created the perception that one of the methods was wrong. Consequently, individuals chose sides—normally along community lines. The much more numerous surface and aviation communities, rather than acknowledging the enormous platform and mission differences and accepting a "different strokes for different folks" philosophy, popularly considered the nuclear submariners to be out of step, like a marcher being off the drum cadence. This out-of-sync condition just doesn't happen unless it's deliberate. It did not take long before the majority of officers in all services viewed nuclear submariners as "bubbleheads" or automatons who blindly followed Rickover's lead.

This view gained credence over time. The public ignored the safety record and listened to those who had been let go for failing to meet the standards (or those who had not even made the initial cut). Since Rickover never explained himself or replied to individuals who had not been accepted for his program or who had been involuntarily released, many in the public came to believe that his process was unfairly punishing otherwise good sailors who failed to "follow the book."[5] Rickover did not answer his critics—so they felt free to write more. His name guaranteed them a headline. But what if Admiral Rickover and his followers were the ones more attentively listening to the beat of modern life?

Driven by the needs of modern manufacturing, commercial organizations in the United States were discovering increased success by establishing and following processes. Whatever the popular jargon of the moment (e.g., "total quality management," "zero defects," "lean manufacturing"), successful industrial managers today are convinced of the importance of capturing individual knowledge (best practices) in processes (written or software documents). Researching the business origin of this concept will lead one back to another Naval Academy graduate, Bill Smith, who, after completing his service commitment, was hired by Motorola. Smith was soon building computer chips for the first mass-produced small calculator and needed his silicon components to have a low probability of failure. He found he could get what was necessary only by rigidly controlling each step of the manufacturing process. His efforts to do so subsequently were documented in the concept known as Six Sigma. A second key figure in this manufacturing revolution was W. Edwards Deming, the American electrical engineer generally credited with starting the quality revolution (*Kaizen*) that so improved Japan's automobile industry (and consequently nearly destroyed the American "Big Three," until Ford hired Deming back from Japan). The third person you will inevitably encounter in your research is Adm. Hyman G. Rickover.

Each of these three was faced with complex engineering projects (calculators for Smith, manufacturing millions of automobiles for Deming, reactors for the third guy). Each realized that a necessary step in achieving his particular goal was to have the supporting industries adopt more exacting engineering standards than had previously been conceived possible. This was possible only through the establishment of demanding standards and a process of continuous improvement. Each man achieved values their peer practitioners had heretofore believed unachievable.

At the same time, both Deming and Rickover recognized the need for innovation.[6] In business this is often characterized as out-of-the-box thinking. Innovation in business is what develops the new product that will someday employ a new industry. In the military, innovation is a way to save lives or win a battle with a new concept. For example, the marriage of the tank and an installed radio enabled the German Wehrmacht to quickly sweep around the Maginot line.[7]

Of course, the people who appreciate the need to follow process may not be the same individuals who embrace innovation. A successful organization needs people with both personality types to coexist and excel. The critical management question is, How in the world should talent be parsed to accomplish both goals?

We have discussed how the nuclear-submarine forces approached this problem. They determined what was routine, established a process to control that action, assigned the routine processes to the junior personnel, and tasked senior managers (expected to be more capable) with innovation. But what happened when a bad process was inadvertently installed and accepted?

An event that occurred while I was in command of a San Diego–based submarine demonstrates how Rickover balanced process and innovation. Around that time Admiral Rickover's staff introduced a new method to check the proper operation of electrical equipment that directly affected the safety of the reactor. The test was termed Operating Instruction 62 (O/I 62). A form of this test had been in place since the beginning of the nuclear-power program, but recently, the process had been changed to make it more comprehensive. Now the procedure routinely checked the integrity of the electrical sensing systems within the reactor plant as well as the supporting electrical plant, including the huge air-cooled breakers Rickover had been personally responsible for designing and installing to prevent battle-shock damage during World War II.[8] Naval Reactors' new test required that all of the major power sources be disconnected and reconnected multiple times.

Consequently, during the five or six hours the procedure required, no electronic equipment could be used throughout the ship (unless one wanted to risk the sensitive equipment being damaged by a dramatic power surge). Since the air-conditioning plants would thus be off for some time and a nuclear submarine is nearly insufferable without air conditioning, it became common practice to do O/I 62 late at night, after the sun had set, the regular workday had finished, and most of the crew had returned safely home. Of course, late at night fewer supervisors were on board, and by that time the men performing O/I 62 had already done a full day's work.

A year or more after the new procedure had been introduced, I heard through the grapevine that while conducting the test on board a ship on the other coast, an electrician had been electrocuted. I wrangled a copy of the investigation. The report was brief and straight-forward. It said that the procedure had been precisely followed, with proper safety supervision present, but the electrician conducting the operation had been careless and permitted his arm to brush against a powered 450-volt copper bus bar. He was killed instantly.

Now, the nuclear-submarine business was particularly dangerous in the early years, and I had by this time already seen several men die on board and around boats. But you know what? No men had ever died when they were being properly supervised. In fact, this is a rule you can wrap up and take to work with you: *People don't die when they are being properly supervised.* I knew the investigation report was wrong, but there are many problems in the world. This one was not mine and was furthermore greater than three thousand miles removed. I cast the report into a locker over my bunk.

Six months later, standing in the San Diego submarine officers' bar, I overheard someone gossiping. Another electrician had been lost while conducting O/I 62. I made an inquiring telephone call and was informed that both the latest death and its subsequent investigation were believed to be none of my business. Nevertheless, the submarine force is small. Within a week an unmarked envelope containing a copy of the official report appeared in my in-box. Surprise, surprise, the account ran along the lines of the earlier one. In short, the junior electrician was properly supervised and everything was in order. All of a sudden the ex-soul foolishly leaned the wrong way and killed himself. Conclusion: no one at fault but the dead guy. Recommended changes: none. None to the procedure. None to the equipment. None to the training. Nobody at fault. Nobody to be held accountable. No one responsible for someone dying.

I remember standing with the latest report in my hand reflecting on my own responsibility. The deaths had occurred someplace else on board other ships (i.e., the accidents were definitely not in my chain of command, or "lane," as civilian organizations might say). I was not even officially aware of the accidents, and furthermore, some officials with the proper responsibility had already decided the deaths had resulted from the deceased's own failures. However, my gut told me both investigations were as flawed as their senior reviewers.

I was in command of a submarine, so I essentially had my own test platform available. And since I was in command of a submarine, unless I checked the procedure myself before the next scheduled O/I 62, I might very well end up shipping the body of one of my young electricians home. I have a personal management rule: *People may not be prepared for the situation in which they find themselves in life. The good leader recognizes this and reassigns them to a place or position where they can be successful. If there is no appropriate role in which they can flourish, the best course of action for all is to sever the relationship. The only clearly wrong decision is to demand that an unprepared person face a challenging climb alone.*

The night I read the second investigation, I walked down to the Goat Locker to ask the senior chief electrician to lend me a hand.[9] I informed him the two of us were going to do O/I 62 that evening. He was going to read the procedure and record results while I took the actual readings. Taking the readings had been the role performed by the two junior electricians who had died.

Within an hour we had laid out rubber safety mats on the submarine steel deck, put up warning signs for the passersby, and commenced. The process moved along about as quickly as expected; it had been years since I had operated the test equipment, and there are always tricks to any trade. The procedure was lengthy and required the removal of heavy steel protective panels to expose live 450-volt bus bars. The latter contained enough voltage to kill anyone, and while the copper was exposed, we took readings from the live bus bars. We repeated the measurements twice more: once after the breakers were tripped open and then again after the bright shiny bars were reenergized. The chief and I then hoisted the heavy steel panel covers back in place and screwed the threaded retainers semitight (we knew the procedure would have us double back to this same location once more) before we moved our safety mats and barriers to a new location. Then we would again establish the prescribed electrical conditions in order to take a new set of readings.

Of course, we were working in one of the main passageways of a submarine, and anyone walking fore or aft might try to squeeze by on the other side of us from the electrically live (charged) network rather than choosing a longer path. But it was late at night, and there was not a great deal of foot traffic. In addition, two people had died, so the chief and I were particularly alert for dangerous situations. The senior chief was one of my best supervisors; in fact, he had monitored this particular evolution every quarter for a couple of years.

Each time the operator in the maneuvering room remotely switched an air-cooled breaker to change the electrical conditions, I would take measurements with a voltmeter to ensure the proper thick copper bars were fully charged or dead. Sometimes the big bars on the right were live, and sometimes it was those on the left, and every now and then it was the ones up high and toward the back of the cabinet. To get the latter readings, I had to stand on my toes and reach deep into the gray steel enclosure.

It was warm on the submarine without any air conditioning, so the senior chief and I both were sweating a bit. We had taken off our long-sleeved uniform shirts and were down to our T-shirts. Four hours into the process, I was convinced the procedure was not particularly complicated, and I was thinking maybe this was a wild goose chase. Perhaps my gut was wrong, and the two investigation reports had been correct. Maybe the men who died were simply careless.

We were now well into the rhythm of things, and I was wondering when might be a good time for a cigarette break. The men in maneuvering reset another group of breakers. The senior chief read me the instructions for the next step. I repeated the guidance to him verbatim, picked up the voltmeter, began to swing back toward the open cabinet, and stopped. For some reason my hips had started to rotate but my arms had not yet moved, and as I looked down, I could see the sweaty hairs of my bare left arm actually reaching straight out for the live bus bar immediately to my left. The high voltage copper and my arm were separated by less than a quarter of an inch. I carefully swayed right and abruptly sat down. The chief wordlessly lit a cigarette, bent over, and stuck it between my teeth. Then he lit one for himself. His hands were shaking. I was sitting on mine. When we finished our cigarettes, the senior chief and I wordlessly lifted the heavy steel panels back into place and screwed them tightly shut. We then went in search of a sheaf of electrical system drawings and a couple of pencils.

Two weeks later, after drilling some holes and installing a couple of hundred dollars' worth of equipment obtained at a local hardware store, we had modified the cabinets. With our slight changes one could read the main bus voltages without removing the safety covers. Our connection design maintained the watertight integrity of the enclosure. Once we had made the alterations, the senior chief and I redid the test to demonstrate that O/I 62 would produce identical results if performed our way. We then removed our changes and did the test the old way (with exceptional care) so that the ship was back to normal.

I submitted our recommended change (a two-and-a-half-inch stack of new processes, procedures, and drawings) via the chain of command. My boss, who would the following year be selected for the rank of admiral, soon called me up to his sea cabin. His lair was on the fifth deck of the large repair ship moored just across the pier from my submarine.

As soon as I was standing at attention in front of his desk, he used the tips of his fingers to slowly push our document across his desk toward me. He accompanied his disdainful gesture with comments that frankly seemed mildly discouraging: "We all know Admiral Rickover is the most renowned electrical engineer in the bureau. We all know he personally designed these breakers being tested and is particularly proud of that achievement. If he says an electrical procedure is safe and correct, I, for one, am not going to challenge him!"

My wife always cautions me that my every emotion is clearly evident in my face. With that in mind, I focused my gaze above the commodore's head. The interior of all Navy surface ships is a mixture of gray, blue, and green. The old Navy adage is "If it doesn't move, paint it." The only pipes not specifically painted on a Navy ship are those formed from copper, for copper doesn't rust. Navy copper pipes are shined. In the commodore's cabin even the wiring cabling was painted gray.

He spoke again, his voice rising, "How dare you make a change to your engineering plant to attempt to prove that something unauthorized would work? Who do you think you are?"

I could see that someone perhaps weary of the penetrating smell of brass polish in an enclosed space, an odor I also have always found offensive, had painted the copper pipes that ran along the overhead of the commodore's office. I wondered if I should inform my commodore that each day he sat down in his big leather chair, he was positioned smack dab beneath an express violation of the Bureau of Ships manual, specifically a footnote contained somewhere in volume 26. I parsed my recollection. I might be wrong; it could be volume 24. In my mind I leafed through the chapters trying to recall.

The commodore abruptly stood. I sensed he was trying to look down on me. I was a wee bit taller, but he was now nearly interrupting my line of sight to the painted copper pipes. Now I was also looking down on a thinning spot beginning to form near the back of the crown of his head. "I am going to forget this, but don't ever do it again!" He sat back down, his right hand swooping his hair back to cover the balding area, his left hand again pushing our pile of papers away from him. The recommended change teetered between the desk edge and the floor.

I decided he didn't want to know about the copper pipe. Besides, I knew how to go about getting a waiver for copper that had already been painted . . . but if I brought that up he would probably just suggest retiring to the officers' club to discuss, over a friendly beer or two, obtaining said permission . . . and I had pressing matters I needed to accomplish that afternoon.

I went back to my ship and asked the yeoman for a mailing box. I dropped the procedure inside, addressed the box to Admiral Rickover at his home, and included a short personal note:

Dear Admiral Rickover,

If you want to stop killing people, read this.

> Very respectfully,
> Dave Oliver
> Captain, US Navy

Once off the base on the way to watch my sons play soccer, I mailed the box. I paid for the postage out of my own pocket. I wasn't sure the commodore would support an expense claim.

I was later informed by my brother, Tim, who was on Rickover's staff at the time, that the day after the mail system delivered my box, Rickover simply brought it in from home and handed it to the head of his electrical section. Rickover asked that it be evaluated—and directed that no one in the electrical section leave work until the assessment was completed (a standard Rickover practice greatly appreciated by those of us who had difficulty getting any of our letters answered by other Navy functional organizations). When the head of the electrical section reported to Rickover that the recommended change was correct, Rickover took several actions, one of which caused me a bit of career grief. The admiral first directed that the change be issued immediately, precisely as the senior chief and I had written.[10] Second, Rickover fired the head of his electrical department. Two men had died, and his electrical head should have picked up on the problems in the investigation reports long before I did. Rickover's sense of personal responsibility was almost always at a perfect pitch. When I later heard about his action, I mentally applauded. Finally, Rickover picked up the telephone and called my commodore.

I later found out that my boss had not been completely honest with me. My commodore had not really "forgotten" what he considered my insubordination. Instead, he had reported my "challenge of Rickover" to his superiors (this word of course had immediately reached Rickover's ears). I fear my commodore might have been firing blindly in the hope that someone really senior in the Navy, preferably the seventy-eight-year-old Admiral Rickover himself, would decide to hammer me for not "following process." Unfortunately for my commodore, Admiral Rickover didn't consider my action a transgression. Instead, the four-star admiral made an alternate "suggestion" to my boss.

I don't recall what I was working on that day when the commodore unexpectedly called my executive officer and requested that all my officers and crew fall in at attention on the pier between our two ships. The commodore said he wanted to speak to everyone. This was an unusual order. In fact, it had never happened before, and he had bypassed the chain of command by calling my exec. Violating a military convention like this was just not his style.

The buzz was big, and everyone moved with alacrity. I don't recall linking this strange occurrence with the cardboard box I had mailed three or four days earlier. I know we had not yet received the new O/I 62 message from Naval Reactors. It was only when the commodore began addressing the crew by saying he wanted everyone to hear his "sincere apologies to their commanding officer" that I sensed the day was not going smoothly.

You see, the hero of our story, Admiral Rickover, was one of those unique individuals who could simply accept that he (or one of his closest advisers) was wrong—even if the issue involved a personal accomplishment in which he had previously taken great pride. When it was determined he was in error, Rickover always looked anew at the evidence, chose a better path, and never looked back. He was the best I have ever seen at accepting correction.

However, Rickover had a different flaw. He accepted direct criticism, and he expected others to be equally grown-up. Unfortunately, most supervisors in the world, including my commodore that day, are not nearly as mature and magnanimous. Few people behave as Rickover did. Most of the time, if the boss or one of his close associates is wrong, the error must be disguised in some costume and called a unicorn—or something equally fanciful—in order for the person who identified the error to survive.

Partially because of this incident, my commodore and I subsequently had a relatively strained relationship. Consequently, I never shared with him my observation about his improperly painted copper piping. Possibly because I failed to offer to buy him an accompanying beer, he subsequently wrote the worst fitness report I received during my thirty-six years in the Navy.[11] Still, I never did ship one of my submariners home in a casket, and no one else in the submarine force subsequently died during O/I 62. It may all have turned out for the best.

———

Earlier in the chapter it was noted that

> the nuclear force had adopted a policy of ruthlessly discriminating between operations that should be treated as ordinary and other work. If the work to be done was judged routine, then it was completed in accordance with precise procedures. These rigid procedures were written to require only a moderate level of talent, training, and supervision to achieve the proper degree of safety. By this careful differentiation between tasks, submarine leadership attention could be

redirected and prioritized to those nonroutine management functions that required special attention, intellect, or innovation.

. . . Throughout Rickover's life and beyond, each day the nuclear submarine became safer and more effective. Continual improvement eventually became the hallmark of the submarine force.

What do you think about this approach to management? Have you seen organizations that manage differently? How do they create an organizational culture that fosters innovation? How do they develop the proper balance between quality and innovation?

12

～

Elephant Instincts

*One must permit his people the freedom to seek added work and
greater responsibility. In my organization, there are no formal job
descriptions or organizational charts. Responsibilities are defined
in a general way, so that people are not circumscribed.
All are permitted to do as they think best and to go to anyone
and anywhere for help. Each person then is limited only
by his own ability.*[1]

No matter how capable, deserved, or well entrenched a particular
leader, another claimant is always waiting just offstage, impatient for a
moment in the spotlight. It would be gracious to say the man or woman
in the wings ascribes to a different vision. But most often they just have
a soul-wrenching need for their own fifteen minutes of recognition, a deep
desire to prove the great pitcher Catfish Hunter's sage observation correct:
"The sun don't shine on the same dog's ass all the time."

To stay in power, leaders need to be effective and also possess the necessary skills to shape and carry each of the important issues. Equally, they
must never ignore the instincts that brought them to the top of the boil. I
do not know how many engagements Admiral Rickover lost. My supposition is they were few and far between. However, I was present one time
when his desires were definitely not observed.

Context is important. This episode happened near the tail end of the
Vietnam War—a particularly difficult time for the Navy and our nation.
Public support for the war was plummeting. That was the external
environment.

Out in the fleet, the Navy was experiencing mini race riots on some of
the carriers and was in the process of recognizing it had an organizational

alcohol problem. In Washington the Navy portion of the Pentagon and Congress were locked in an acrimonious public debate about how much of the surface Navy should be nuclear powered (nuclear power plants were more capable than petroleum-based ones but also more expensive). Since money is always both constrained and fungible, for many this was simply an argument over whether there should be more or fewer ships.

Elmo Zumwalt, the youngest Chief of Naval Operations in U.S. history, had been appointed to lead the Navy. Many thought he had been selected because of the racial problems in the service (the Navy was still effectively segregated), material failures (the surface fleet had not been replaced or revitalized following hard service in three wars—World War II, Korea, and Vietnam), and the dismal morale caused by senior naval leaders with mores and attitudes toward junior personnel more appropriate to the previous century.

Armed with immense self-confidence, Zumwalt quickly made many changes. Like most disturbances to the status quo, his "Z-grams" were in general despised by the conservative Navy leadership (no matter how much the same modifications were admired by many younger officers and enlisted personnel). Two of his most important cultural changes involved desegregating the Navy and introducing women on board Navy ships and aircraft. Demonstrating his multidimensional capabilities, after he had retired, Zumwalt would run (unsuccessfully) as a Democrat to represent Virginia in the U.S. Senate and subsequently become the president of the American Medical Building Corporation.

The Secretary of the Navy (and Marine Corps) was John Warner, then married to Elizabeth Taylor—the same Ms. Taylor who was probably the most famous movie star of her age. Secretary Warner would subsequently become Senator Warner from Virginia and eventually chairman of the Senate Armed Services Committee. He was a Republican and not personally enamored with Admiral Zumwalt, who returned this sentiment. It was the era of Vietnam, Watergate, and larger-than-life personalities in the Navy. It was a superb time to be in our nation's capital, and I was fortunate enough to have a ticket to a seat in the wings on stage left.[2] I had gotten there essentially by winning the lottery.

My particular sweepstakes day began one early morning in a dry dock floating in the Thames River near New London, Connecticut. A few unusually large ships in the U.S. Navy serve their lives as floating dry docks. Those I was familiar with were constructed by welding large steel-plate Us together until a length sufficient to handle the largest submarine was formed. Then a bow was riveted to one end. At the opposite end two large gates powerful enough to swing wide open, yet be watertight when shut, completed the ship.

Dry docks are designed to be flooded far enough down in a river or bay for the submarine to be brought over the sill by a combination of thick hawsers and precisely maneuvered tugs. If you haven't done this, trust me, it is a very dicey evolution in any sort of wind or tide. The ship is slowly pulled into the dock until the submarine is precisely positioned atop newly cut spruce timber caps, which will gently crush as they absorb the submarine's weight, thus compensating for minor hull imperfections. At this point the dry-dock gates are hauled shut, the lights flicker, and the immense dry-dock pumps begin spewing acres of water over the side. The dry dock and the submarine inside begin their perceptible ascent from the brine. Within a few hours after the submarine has entered dry dock, repair work begins on areas of the boat that often haven't been accessible for months or perhaps even years. The frantic work pace is accompanied by the putrid smell of the millions of dying organisms that attached themselves below the waterline while the ship was floating.

At one period in my life, I spent more than my share of time in dry dock. I did so not by choice but because of three things: a fact, a tradition, and an observation. The fact was that USS *Nautilus*, the world's first nuclear submarine, had twin screws. This was not unusual. Most diesel submarines had two propellers. Our problem was the odd placement of the screws. To squeeze our destroyer-escort engine room into a diesel-submarine hull, our propulsion shafts had been angled out a bit from centerline. As a result, the outside arc of the screw blades extended a few inches beyond the widest girth of our ship. Consequently, the tips of each blade were the first part of the ship to make contact if we were not terribly careful as we approached a pier.

In addition, because the angled shafts produced a disproportionately small effective rotational moment arm, even with a powerful nuclear reactor we could not get nearly the stationary rotational power a normal diesel boat generated. Unfortunately, tradition demanded that two-screwed ships, as *Nautilus* surely was, not deign to use tugs to assist them in berthing or getting under way.[3] Using tugs had been considered a social sin among diesel submariners, and that bias accompanied them to the nuclear ships.

And finally, the observation: My commanding officer at that time was the most challenged ship handler with whom I ever served. This was not entirely his fault. He apparently had an undetected severe medical condition—an enlarged hubris. He thought he understood relative motion better than God. Consequently, our moving steel vessel more than kissed many stationary objects.

Because all three conditions (bad design, unthinking diesel practice carryover, and excessive hubris) coexisted on *Nautilus'* bridge, I became experienced with dry docks. To replace inexplicably (at least to our commanding officer) battered screws, we entered these large steel beasts on multiple occasions. But that particular night I lay underneath the three thousand tons of steel that was *Nautilus*, back braced against one of the enormous wooden keel blocks, my submarine sweater and ugly green foul-weather coat only partially shielding me from the cold, not because of another dinged screw. I was there, for the fourth time in the last year, trying to figure out why some very large valves wouldn't operate properly.

I had been engineer officer on board *Nautilus* for three full years. I had solved a number of long-standing problems. We no longer averaged a fire a day and two reactor scrams a week. I had done well enough that in the morning I was flying to Washington, D.C., as one of the three finalists for the position of first fellow to the Chief of Naval Operations. Thus, I had only two more hours (if I intended to take a shower—and the smell of the dying shellfish clinging to my skin probably made this a necessity) to determine how to make the main circulating water valves close without excessive torque, something I had never seen them do before.

It was nearly three in the morning, and I had been out of ideas for hours, if not months. I had told everyone else to hit the rack at midnight. I was simply being stubborn now. All that remained in the dry dock was me, an eight-cell flashlight, half a pack of Pall Malls, and my pride. I shifted my butt atop a nest of crushed shells. The prick of the shells and the putrid smell (I still can't eat mussels) were the only things that had kept me awake the last two hours because after the early sundown the New England temperature had plunged well below freezing.

When *Nautilus* was at sea, tons of water a second coursed through the main circulating pipes to cool the steam produced by the nuclear reactor. These pipes were the most egregious flooding threat in the ship. The submarine *Thresher* had perished a few years earlier from a problem with a much smaller pipe. To compensate for this danger, these sixteen-inch-wide pipes were guarded by huge valves designed to be closed, even against the entire pressure of the ocean deep, within seconds. These very valves had been pulled from the ship and now lay on the smelly shells before me. I certainly did not want to leave the ship in this condition, but the officer who was to relieve me (Dick Fast) had already reported on board, and only a few hours were left before my flight to Washington, D.C. I was down to simply taunting myself.

I idly played the beam of the flashlight on the nearest valve. The large metal shape lay on its side in the dry dock a couple of feet from me, the shadows of the dock lighting interplaying with the beam from my flash-light. I lit another cigarette from the butt of the one I was smoking and flicked the old one at the valve in disgust. It hit in a flash of sparks. Instead of dropping among the inflammable debris of the broken shells, it fell into a valve crevice.

I wearily got to my feet to fish the butt out. As my index and mid-dle fingers felt for the cigarette, they rubbed against the operating piston shank, and I realized there was something embossed on the shaft. I traced the discontinuity, trying to visualize what I was feeling. I could swear it was two small letters. My flashlight was no help, so I wet my fingers and rubbed again. It felt very much like an *R* and an *H*. I closed my weary eyes, and when I opened them, I was looking back at the large stern gates of the dry dock. Was it possible? Maybe.

I moved over to the starboard side to check the two valves that lay on the deck there. Using my penknife to scrape away the verdigris, I quickly also found raised letters on that shank. These I could see: "LH."

After climbing the six levels of ladders up from the floor of the dry dock, I woke the four men of the M-Gang, sending them down into the dock to reassemble the circulating water valves and test them. Before I took a shower and changed into my service dress blues, I checked Machinery History, which at that period contained a record of every evolution per-formed with a ship's equipment since the ship's keel had been laid. In a cou-ple of minutes, I found a pertinent penciled ten-year-old entry: "Removed, cleaned and replaced the main circ water valves, K. R. McKee."

I took a quick shower as Linda, my wife and also my ride to the air-port, was already waiting at the head of the pier. Before boarding the air-plane I called back to the ship. The valves had already been swapped to the opposite sides (right hand [RH] / left hand [LH]—we were not very sophis-ticated in those days and had a ways to go on part interchangeability), greased, and reinstalled in the ship. They were now opening and shutting with less than 10 percent of the dry torque previously required. It looked as if an ancient problem had been solved.

I slept the entire thirty-minute shuttle across the Long Island Sound and, after changing planes in New York City, on the ninety-minute flight to Washington.

In the interview process to become the Navy's first Chief of Naval Operations fellow, I believe I finished third out of three candidates. I certainly didn't finish first. I may have slipped to second when Admiral Zumwalt, the first uniformed four-star admiral I ever met, poured me a cup of coffee, handed it to me, and said, "How is Linda?" I only looked at him quizzi-cally. After an uncomfortable silence, he continued, "Linda, your wife?"

Instead of coolly replying, "Fine, and how is Mouza?"[4] I reflexively jerked and tipped my coffee on the wide gold stripes covering his sleeves from his cuffs nearly to his elbows.

Although that meeting was admittedly a bit uneven, it was not the worst interview I had that day. Three hours earlier I had taken a cab from National Airport for my very first visit to the Pentagon. We were in our seventh year of war in Vietnam. Nixon was president, and Watergate was looming. The antiwar and antiestablishment movement was in full bloom. Uniformed men had been known to have blood or paint thrown on them as they came to and from work. As a result, everyone working at the Pentagon, except the most senior officers (those assigned their own cars and drivers), wore civilian clothes, except on Wednesdays (a halfhearted effort to ensure everyone in Washington still owned a uniform) or on days they went to Capitol Hill to testify. That Monday, when I walked into a poorly lit Pentagon office for a preinterview, it was impossible for me to tell if I was meeting a civilian or an officer. Since the first individual with whom I met was wearing a suit, I assumed he was a civilian.

As I started to sit down across from him, I noticed his name, printed on a cheap plastic laminate plate and slid into a wooden triangular holder on his desk: K. R. McKee. Instead of continuing the slide down into my seat, I reared up and stepped back, my voice rising a bit: "Are you the K. R. McKee who was on board *Nautilus* in 1961? The one who was unable to get the main circ water valves installed back on the correct sides?" Perhaps the previous evening, as well as the stress of several years of trying to fix this exasperating situation, was still fresh on my mind.

Yes, even upon reflection years later, I think that half hour with Capt. Kin McKee, Admiral Zumwalt's personal friend and perhaps his most trusted adviser, was by far the low point of that particular day. A few months later McKee became an admiral himself, and he eventually became the next Admiral Rickover, when Rickover himself retired—so perhaps I could have better chosen someone with whom to pick a fight my first day in Washington.[5]

However, that evening, while I was dejectedly waiting to board my plane to return to Connecticut, the Bureau of Personnel had me paged at the airport. Kin was looking for a submarine officer for his own staff. As a result, while I spectacularly failed the interview to be the Navy's first fellow,[6] I was soon busy performing special projects for Kin McKee and his friend and boss, Admiral Zumwalt. For two years my responsibilities involved tasks such as smuggling arms to Israel (a skirting of the law that I assume is long past the appropriate statute of limitations), recommending mining Hanoi Harbor to change the course in Vietnam, developing the first submarine cruise missile (more successful than the mining), and coordinating with the State Department. Most of these bits and pieces are beyond the range of this book, but what is definitely within scope is my frequent service as the communication path between the two Navy giants of the day: Adm. Elmo R. Zumwalt Jr. and Adm. Hyman G. Rickover.

I thought they were both extraordinary. The Navy was fortunate to have these two visionary leaders, for just as Admiral Rickover could see well into the future, Admiral Zumwalt had an equivalent gift. Each was innovative and ingenious and drove cultural change but went about accomplishing his goals much differently, in a manner best suited to his own personality and the time he had available. Rickover built an organization that could develop the necessary cultural change over decades. He worked many details himself. He was an introvert and did not enjoy charming large audiences. In contrast, Zumwalt inherited a Navy that badly needed immediate and dramatic transformation, and he had only four years to accomplish this change. He also understood why he had been selected over nearly a hundred of his seniors to become the youngest Chief of Naval Operations in history. He was a public charmer and burned with an energy that threatened to outshine the sun.[7]

Surrounded by fellow admirals and political leaders who (to be charitable) thought everything was just fine, Admiral Zumwalt believed that the Navy of the early seventies was racist and unnecessarily elitist. He was convinced that the service needed a cultural change. Effecting this change was not an easy job, for Zumwalt was not leading a band of admirers. Many in Congress and certainly a large number of Navy officers did not see any reason to alter the current course. Zumwalt realized, however, that not only was the Navy's existing position morally bankrupt, but the service would not survive if it remained unable to attract black, Hispanic, and female recruits—and it wasn't going to do it with its disgraceful reputation. Correctly identifying recruiting of minorities as his most important priority, Admiral Zumwalt turned his attention away from the management of the naval aspects of the Vietnam War (a task he handed to Kin McKee) and began with a bang the efforts to force change.[8]

Reflecting the larger Navy's antipathy, Zumwalt's successors reversed many of his alterations soon after he had retired. Nevertheless, the mere spark of an unsuccessful revolution is often sufficient to breed other revolutionaries, and Zumwalt broke some ancient glass that could not be replaced, no matter how hard fools later tried. The course of our Navy was inevitably altered for the better as a result of Admiral Zumwalt's stewardship. But as the classic writers remind us, our heroes are not always perfect, and one of my heroes—Admiral Zumwalt—had a visceral negative reaction to another of mine—Admiral Rickover.[9] Displaying exceptional judgment, Kin McKee wisely stood back from the line of fire and left me to carry volleys from the Pentagon (where Admiral Zumwalt held sway) to Crystal City (Admiral Rickover's den), three miles away.

Contrary to public opinion at the time, in the several exchanges I personally witnessed, Admiral Rickover was professional and courteous in his public and private demeanor with Admiral Zumwalt. My observation, however, was definitely not the majority view in Washington at the time. Admiral Zumwalt was good looking and charming, and politically he was much more connected than the cantankerous Rickover. Zumwalt was a Vietnam War hero to the public and Congress. He was also the anointed Navy leader, and he certainly understood how to work a crowd. Zumwalt hit the long ball in the sphere of public relations. Like other leaders of his style, he had an ego that demanded the entire Navy stage. He was not interested in ceding even a back corner to Rickover.

Rickover could not keep pace with Zumwalt. I don't think he could have even if he had had an equivalently large staff. While often in the news, Admiral Rickover made his appearances in civilian clothes and often in a lecturing mode—not quite the same as capturing converts with sparkling blue eyes and a uniform adorned with broad gold stripes and shiny medals. Rickover didn't do sparkling, and his own *Time* cover was sixteen years old.[10]

In some Washington political arenas, it wasn't substance that counted, but style, and in addition to having great substance, Zumwalt was the king of style. He captured the press and rather enjoyed turning the media against Rickover. It may not have been "fair," but personal characteristics grease many a path, and Zumwalt was much more charming than his opponent. Thus, Zumwalt carried the public relations day. As one of Rickover's critics (rather grudgingly) later said, "As a prime exponent of the 'never explain, never complain' school of leadership . . . Rickover projected a more arrogant and arbitrary image than he probably deserved."[11] In the Washington arena Rickover and Zumwalt were galvanizing figures. Most officers chose to ally themselves with one or the other. From my great vantage point, I admired them both.

A few months after I arrived in Washington, the decision was made to build the Trident (formerly the Underwater Launched Missile System [ULMS][12]) submarine. This submarine would be a remarkable step forward. It would be invulnerable. It would carry much-longer-range missiles with maneuverable reentry warheads. Each could reach Soviet targets from as far away as U.S. ports (thus simultaneously increasing U.S. security and possibly making the Air Force Minuteman fields redundant—there is nothing like a little interservice rivalry). The initial base to support these ships would be built on the Pacific coast near Bangor, Washington. In the final Navy decision meeting in the Pentagon with Secretary John Warner, Admiral Zumwalt supported going ahead as planned, but as we adjourned the meeting, the admiral crooked his finger at Kin McKee.

Shortly thereafter, I received a call to report to McKee's office in Rosslyn. He slid a copy of the briefing slides over to my side of the table. "Take a billion dollars out of the Trident program," he said. A billion dollars was a lot of money then (equivalent to about $5 billion today) and was about a quarter of the cost of the entire program just presented and supposedly approved. I hadn't even had a chance to sit down. It didn't appear that we were ever going to finish our discussion about the *Nautilus*' main circulating water valve placement.

McKee provided his typically terse guidance: "The CNO [Chief of Naval Operations, that is, Admiral Zumwalt] agrees we need Tridents, but he still wants money for his new surface ships."[13] A single sheet of paper slid across McKee's desk and nudged the briefing slides. "That should get you in the door." The paper was on the Chief of Naval Operations' personal letterhead and simply stated, "Provide LCDR Oliver whatever assistance he requests." Across the bottom the signature was scrawled: "E. R. Zumwalt."

So, I went around Crystal City knocking on doors and making friends with various submarine admirals who had the mistaken impression their program was already approved at the highest levels. They did not appear overjoyed to find a young officer, armed only with a rather creased note from the Chief of Naval Operations (I should have put it in an envelope instead of my breast pocket), asking to examine everything they had already considered in the design of the ship, reactor plant, missile, and base. Some reacted rather harshly. For example, when I entered the Navy's Special Projects Office, which had, against all odds, managed the building of the Navy's Polaris underwater missiles and which would be responsible for the Trident missiles, a captain whose name I do not recall pinned me up against the reception area wall with his forearm against my throat and described his rather intimate relationship with my mother. I do remember there was an admiral behind him nodding his own firm agreement with everything being screamed in my ear. I also recall deciding I would have to work this issue a bit more delicately. And I recollect that Admiral Rickover calmly instructed his (visibly snarling) staff to fully cooperate with my review before he turned his attention to other matters.

After I had submitted my recommendations to McKee, I next saw my report with the billion dollars in suggested decrements when it had the blue-inked words "Approved, E. R. Zumwalt" scrawled across the cover page.[14]

Neither Admiral Rickover nor anyone from his office ever offered a word of complaint about this decision. Overall resource allocation was within the bailiwick of the Chief of Naval Operations, and Rickover had no intention of rising to the bait of questioning what Caesar's was to decide. I suspect Rickover was the only person in Washington not holding his breath, waiting for the clash. Rickover conserved his energy and focused on the goal of building a sufficient number of attack submarines.

But Rickover's public acquiescence was not sufficient for Zumwalt. The Chief of Naval Operations' antipathy for Rickover was both personal and professional. Since submarines were the primary Cold War thrust against the Soviet Union and their building rate was supported by the president, Zumwalt couldn't mount a direct assault on the submarine building rate. He confined himself to more indirect thrusts, as the following story illustrates:

In the development of nuclear submarines, the nuclear power plant had provided much more underwater speed for submarines, and just as it is for an aircraft platform, speed is life for submarines. However, to go fast—and to avoid the noise from cavitation (air bubbles forming and collapsing as the moving screw blade tips create localized low-pressure areas and collapsing bubbles)—the submarine needs to be able to go deep enough so that the water pressure suppresses cavitation. The limiting depth is driven by the strength of steel in the hull. From diesel boats to present-day boats, the submarine hull has continuously evolved. The steel needs to have many characteristics but, in particular, must be ductile and tough (to absorb depth-charge shock). Equally important, the hull steel needs to be able to be formed and welded into place by individuals who often are not working in the most pristine of conditions.

Submarine hulls have a sordid history of cracks that develop over time. These cracks are caused by stresses that were sealed into the steel when the shipyard welding conditions or process were not exactly right. In some cases new machines had to be developed to avoid the problem. In others the steel being welded had to be held at a particular elevated temperature. Over the years we learned a great deal about working with esoteric steels through trial and error. By the time Admiral Zumwalt became Chief of Naval Operations, submarines had proceeded from high-tensile-strength steel (*Nautilus*) to HY-80 (*George Washington Carver*), and many people were advocating using the much stronger HY-130. The new steel would definitely provide better safety margins. The question was whether it would also bring the same sort of welding challenges we had initially faced with HY-80. Most experts believed the answer was yes.

To avoid excessive development costs and to test the new steel on a smaller scale than in an actual submarine, Rickover had advocated building the NR-2, a small nuclear-powered underwater research vessel (a predecessor, NR-1, was already in operation) with a hull made out of HY-130. Naval Reactors believed that building the NR-2 would help to work out all the welding bugs before the Navy committed to an expensive launch of a new class of submarines. The NR-2 was included in the shipbuilding budget Congress was in the process of reviewing in 1973.

About this time Admiral Rickover had his second heart attack. He was being cared for on the ninth floor of Bethesda Naval Hospital. The Sunday evening after the attack, Admiral Zumwalt and his senior aide, Don Pringle, visited Rickover. As later related to me by Pringle, when the Chief of Naval Operations walked into his room, Admiral Rickover rolled out of bed and began pulling various catheters from his arms.

"What are you doing, Rick? Get back in bed!" Zumwalt exclaimed.

"If you are here, you have figured out a way to screw the submarine force. You only came to make sure I was really dying. I need to get up."

Zumwalt and the nurse eventually convinced Rickover to get back into bed. The Chief of Naval Operations spent thirty minutes in the room, in one of the longest conversations he ever had with Rickover, sitting in a chair he pulled up to the bed.

I heard about this discussion later that evening when Don Pringle called me from Admiral Zumwalt's car, on its way down Wisconsin Avenue from the hospital:[15] "Dave, Admiral Rickover really is going to be in the hospital for at least a couple of weeks. The CNO wants you to go over to the Hill tomorrow and kill the NR-2."

Admiral Rickover had great instincts, as all elephants must have, but he was weak from his heart attack. The NR-2 was never funded by Congress.[16]

The following year I was back working full time in the submarine force. If Rickover knew or suspected that I had assisted his very public enemy (Zumwalt), who was now retired from the Navy (and thus relatively powerless), in cancelling the NR-2, he never mentioned it. In fact, a few years later he bent one of his most sacred rules to keep me eligible for promotion to admiral.

The Navy is supposedly an autocratic organization. Yet both Rickover and Zumwalt were senior leaders who deliberately and forcefully instituted cultural change in the Navy. Rickover completely succeeded. Zumwalt made progress.[17] Is it possible to compare and contrast the different methods that Admiral Zumwalt and Admiral Rickover used to institute cultural change? What methods were effective? Why? Why not? Could either admiral have benefited from one or more of the other's techniques?

Admiral Rickover did not retire for another nine years after the incident with NR-2. By that time he was eighty-two. When he did retire, many of his admirers believed he had stayed beyond his best years.[18] Should his political loss to Admiral Zumwalt over the (non)building of the research submarine have indicated to Rickover that it was time to seek a more physically vigorous man for the job of defending Navy nuclear safety? Do you think Rickover resisted this path simply because Zumwalt was one of his strongest critics? How do leaders recognize when their moment to depart is drawing nigh?

13

Genetics

The Devil is in the details, but so is salvation.[1]

N early everyone who has bought or sold a house understands the secret to real estate success—location, location, location. There is an equivalent in good management—focus, focus, focus. Hyman Rickover made a mantra of this secret. And goodness could he execute. He always focused on what was essential. And he knew what tools he needed: capable people and a system that coaxed the best from them.

I have already discussed Rickover's deep personal investment in the selection of capable people. The admiral was similarly involved in their training. He selected the instructors for all his schools, approved the curriculum, and made periodic visits to the sites. In addition, he paid particular attention to the individuals who filled two specific roles on board his submarines: the engineer and the commanding officer. These individuals were responsible for the technical decisions about the reactor when at sea and frequently operated in radio silence. Rickover insisted on having the final personal approval of any assignment to these two roles, and he required both men to undergo additional testing before they assumed their jobs. To ensure standards didn't slip, the final testing and interviews were performed at Rickover's headquarters in Washington, D.C.

Like all the other training in his program, the testing done at Naval Reactors was a combination of written and oral questions. These weren't examinations for the weak. Eight hours was allotted for the written and more time was often needed; I did not fully complete either of the two written tests I took. The oral testing followed and was performed by the same engineering staff members who had written the textbooks. Orals were always more difficult. They focused on exploring weaknesses or uncertainties evident in the test taker's written answers. These orals could drag out to three or more hours. The standards were absolute and relative: relative because officers with more experience were expected to be equivalently more knowable and nuanced; absolute because if the testing exposed knowledge, temperament, or judgment fissures deemed too wide to be quickly bridged, no matter how long the candidates had been in the program, the individuals were diverted to careers not in submarines. Of the test takers, 10 to 30 percent failed the engineer's examination, and after nearly two decades in the nuclear-power program, some senior officers still stumbled during the commanding officer's testing.

It is important to note that qualified individuals were not deliberately failed. Instead, the failures, at either the engineer level or the commanding officer level (speaking only for the many cases in which I personally knew the individual), were instances of unqualified individuals who, rather than being pushed along until they reached a level of incompetence, were earlier fairly judged and found wanting. In many cases these individuals were intellectually more than qualified but not emotionally well matched with submarine life, just as Rickover had not been. The numbers of failures were small, but the possibility of not passing tended to peg the angst meters of the group being examined. No matter our outward confidence, many of us secretly fear we will prove not good enough.

The first examination (the engineer's) was taken by all nuclear-trained officers interested in continuing their career in submarines. The testing took place three or four years after the officer began nuclear training. The officer either prepared himself (the rule in the earlier years) or was assisted in getting ready. The typical successful officer took the commanding officer's examination ten or twelve years later. This test was reserved for those few individuals who had survived the attrition of time and life's challenges and were deemed worthy to be afloat commanders.[2] This technical assessment was preceded by three months of refresher training at the Naval Reactors headquarters.

Rickover had a good reason for this extra-special attention to the commanding officer, for this individual has always had a particularly unique role in the Navy. In literature, when an author needs to display the impact an absolute despot can have on the minds and souls of others, the narrator often stages his scenes on a ship at sea. The narrative of the story is driven by the captain's character flaw (*Caine Munity*'s Captain Queeg,

Captain Bligh on *Bounty*, or of course, Captain Ahab on board *Pequod*). Rickover did his best to ensure he got rid of most of the twisted souls. If the occasional one slipped through, then that egomaniac was going to at least understand the principles of nuclear power.

When I attended my prospective commanding officer course in 1977, the training reviewed each of the engineering areas we had been expected to assimilate during our careers, with seminars and written examinations every couple of weeks. While the size of the class depended on the need in the fleet, most often it consisted of less than a dozen officers. The three months culminated in the normal eight-hour written and four-hour oral examination, followed by a session with Admiral Rickover.[3]

During our course of training, we were assigned small two-person cubicles for study. I had rented an apartment nearby so I could spend time with my family at nights during the last days of summer before they all went back to school in San Diego. Candidly, I believed I could afford the time as I had much more engineering experience than most of my peers. Possibly some of this impression was based on wishful thinking, as I hadn't seen Linda or our sons, David and Morgan, much in the previous three years, when I was deployed to the Western Pacific, and I was determined to squeeze in time with them while everyone else in my group was studying. Possibly part of my evaluation was based on watching my cubicle mate's progress. He had never served in an engineer billet. If he made it through this course, I judged it was going to be by only a razor-thin margin.

I learned that his family was solidly southern—South of Broad Street, if you have ever been in Charleston, South Carolina (or read Pat Conroy). He had graduated from the Citadel in Charleston and married a local belle. He and his wife lived three blocks from both of their ancestral homes, and he had a drawl that could *not* be cut with a sharp knife. He was on his way to command a ballistic-missile submarine (this assignment had an accompanying lesser opportunity for a "major medal"—nearly essential if one was considered to be in the competition for promotion to admiral—than did an attack submarine but also involved much less stress). He could not have been happier. The ship was homeported in Charleston, and his family wouldn't have to move. I remember thinking that I did not know when I had met a more iconic southern gentleman.

Soon it was time for our final interview with Admiral Rickover. He had decided to speak with us as a group. Ten study desks had been pushed together, side to side, in a small room. We were all wearing suits and ties, as we did each day at Naval Reactors. I was squeezed into the center, my cubicle mate at my left. Everyone in the room was apprehensive. We all had worked long and hard to be selected for command, and none of us wanted to lose this opportunity on the last day. We also knew the admiral was a high-energy person.

Most of the students there had not spoken to Rickover since he had interviewed them twenty years earlier. We knew, but had not yet internalized, we were about to begin frequently communicating with him. Rickover required periodic letters from his commanding officers and was in the habit of episodically calling each nuclear-ship commanding officer. The worst-case phone call was when one of Rickover's agents had reported something noteworthy, and the commanding officer, caught flat-footed, tried to think on his feet and improvise an explanation without knowing the details.

Because of my engineer's tour on board *Nautilus* and the engineering difficulties we had experienced during the *Haddo* overhaul in Pascagoula, I had spoken professionally with the Old Man several times over the years, so I already knew the secret (never, never make anything up). As I looked around the room that day, I realized I was probably the exception. Although it was October, the room was hot—perhaps from the sweating students. Capt. Zack Pate, our instructor, didn't appear particularly nervous.[4] Suddenly, Rickover entered, both his hands pushing us back down in our seats as we respectfully rose.

The admiral, hands clasped behind his back, his eyes on the wooden floor, began to slowly pace back and forth in front of the small room. He was short enough that nearly half his body seemed to disappear each time he passed behind the instructor's desk in the middle of the room. I hadn't seen him in three or four years, and his body had continued to shrink from what was not a very imposing size at his zenith. He must have just barely been able to pass the Naval Academy entry requirement . . . after fifty-seven years of service . . . my thoughts broke off as he finally stopped pacing and looked up.

"If one of you makes a mistake, I'll understand." His voice was almost soothing, instead of the high-pitched bark I had heard before. "I know the pressures you are under."

He clasped his hands back together and returned to his slow pace. We students were pushed so close together, I could feel my cubicle mate actually begin to relax. I glanced over at him and realized that not only was he starting to smile, his lower jaw was moving. He was chewing gum. I had been studying and drinking beer with a man who did not understand the essence of survival in the nuclear world.

First of all, relaxing was a huge mistake. Admiral Rickover never gave a damn about the pressures anyone was under—ever. My cubicle mate should have known that the admiral was making a verbal feint. Rickover was fond of noting that no one goes home to the wrong spouse in the evening. He believed every individual's responsibility to maintain nuclear safety was much more important than family relationships, so woe be to the person who made an error and then attempted to explain the mistake away by saying he or she was tired or under pressure. The only standard acceptable to Rickover was for everything to be done correctly every time.

Secondly, Rickover hated gum. He thought people who chewed gum were, at best, sociopaths.

Finally, return to rule one: never relax around a badger or an admiral. I respected this man more than anyone except my father, but he was still Admiral Rickover. My eyes went back to the center of the room. Rickover had stopped pacing. He was now standing behind the instructor's desk looking with fascination at my cubicle mate's masticating lower jaw. The admiral continued with his metaphor: "If you make a mistake, I'll understand because I've studied genetics."

I ventured a quick glance around the room. The only one who didn't have a quizzical look on his face was Zack, and Zack's eyes were willing me to look back at the admiral—as if we both didn't know precisely what was coming next. I knew the hole to which this particular badger was returning. The admiral had been delivering versions of this same message for a quarter of a century: *You are each personally responsible for reactor safety. There are no exceptions.* Hell, I had myself heard him deliver the same message for fifteen years. What did anyone think we were about to hear? There are eight commandments—the Father of the Nuclear Navy has decided to drop a couple?

The admiral smiled as he looked around the room at his charges. Some of them were uncertainly smiling back. He repeated, "I understand genetics. If you make a mistake with my nuclear plant"—his voice began winding up the scale to the slightly unpleasant high pitch that is more normal for him—"it's because your mother was a street whore who trawled for tricks with a mattress on her back."

I cast a quick glance to my left. My cubicle mate's face had turned harsh red, and his gum was now being savaged. I could sense the bottom guy in our class was on the verge of rising to say something in defense of his mother's Southern Honor. I laughed. It sounded rather loud in the small room.

The admiral was instantly standing on my desk, my tie in his hand, pulling my head up toward his. His face was redder than my study mate's. His voice elevated even above the high pitch I remembered: "Did you find something I said particularly funny?"

I simultaneously became aware of two things. First, there was a seventy-seven-year-old man who had suffered at least two heart attacks standing on my desk. Second, I was terrified, a bit sad for someone who liked to think of himself as a battle-hardened warrior. However, while Admiral Rickover is standing on your desk, pulling your tie tight around your throat, it is definitely not the time for excessive self-reflection. My life as I knew it was effectively over unless I responded both appropriately and quickly. I gave it a shot.

"Admiral, I have heard you deliver nearly the identical message about personal responsibility toward reactor safety many times, but I have never heard you say it more entertainingly."

After a long unblinking stare into my eyes, he dropped my tie, jumped directly down from my desk (without touching anything), and walked wordlessly from the room. My classmates politely looked everywhere except at me (did they suspect we were being monitored by some secret camera?). Pate glanced at me for a moment, slightly shook his head, cleared his throat, and announced, "Last day, gentlemen, make sure your cubicles are cleaned out."

While the room cleared, I estimated the height of my desk. I personally didn't understand it. Even if I kept my weight down, there was simply no way I would ever be able to make that leap when I was nearly eighty.

How important is the leader of the organization? Do you believe managers subconsciously convey concepts and leadership principles by their every action?

Admiral Rickover had dual mantras: "The devil is in the details" and "Do what is right." He continually drove all in his organization to accept responsibility and to recognize they were working for a higher purpose.

Do you believe the leader bears absolute responsibility when something goes wrong? When problems occurred in your organization, were the leaders at the top held accountable?

14

Never Beat a Compass So True

Do not regard loyalty as a personal matter.
A greater loyalty is one to the Navy or to the Country.[1]

I f you are ever in the vicinity of Groton, Connecticut, I recommend a visit to the Submarine Museum. The museum is sited directly across the road from the main entrance to the submarine base. The historical buildings are tucked into gentle hills that another mile upriver rise to what is now labeled on the maps as Allyn Mountain but was known in years past as Mount Decatur. The original name stemmed from 1812, as Allyn Mountain was where Adm. Stephen Decatur's sailors constructed a rock-walled fort and anchored the heavy chain on the north side of the Thames River. The chain was to prevent British rowers from towing their heavy gunned ships, wintering a few miles away in New York Harbor, upriver to reach Decatur's small fleet.

Groton, in addition to being surrounded by national historical sites like Fort Decatur, is the only place in the United States where you can tour a nuclear submarine. Here USS *Nautilus* (less her uranium reactor, which years ago was entombed in Hanford, Washington) "floats" in concrete.

Simply driving on I-95 by Groton brings back *Nautilus* memories for me. But mine are not recollections of when *Nautilus* was the queen of the seas—dazzling the entire world with American technology, setting the Soviets back on their heels, and reestablishing American pride after the embarrassment of the Soviet Union being first to put a satellite and a man in space. No, I walked on board *Nautilus* in 1969, after she had been operated without proper maintenance for fifteen years—or as the horse-man's phrase goes, "ridden hard and put away wet" too many times. When I knew *Nautilus*, the boat needed several bottles of extra liniment to pre-vent her from pulling up embarrassingly lame several years before the end of her planned service.

Most officers who served on board *Nautilus* looked on their tour in this ship as the high point of their careers. Not I. For me, Gwen Verdon's sultry musical tones—"Whatever Lola wants, Lola gets"—seem to reso-nate from each steel strut of what was at one time called the Gold Star Bridge.[2] When I was in New London, *Nautilus'* sobriquet was "Lola."[3] The comparison was apt. The diva of the stage and the siren of the sea both demanded inordinate attention. During the three years I dedicated to *Nautilus*, my shipmates selflessly sacrificed their families and personal lives to fix the ship for those who would follow us. My team's experience was particularly difficult, dangerous, and downright unpleasant. I remember Lola well.

Ten years after my *Nautilus* tour, a decade that witnessed another three generations in submarine technology development, I was the com-manding officer of a much newer nuclear submarine in the Pacific. We had been at sea for most of the last three years and were now beginning an overhaul at the nation's premier shipyard. I had never been in the Puget Sound Naval Shipyard at Bremerton, Washington, but the situation looked to me a lot like the one in New London. This time the crux of the problem wasn't the first nuclear submarine but rather the first nuclear cruiser (USS *Long Beach*), which was being simultaneously overhauled along with the first nuclear carrier, USS *Enterprise*.

The situation in Bremerton was even more difficult than the *Nautilus* problem had been. Bremerton was normally efficient precisely because of its large size. The engineering duty officers and the civilian trade-shop stewards who managed the yard were able to shift people and their skills around as necessary to address the complexities of a varied workload. In fact, while several American shipyards could handle only one or two nuclear submarines, Bremerton had proved it could overhaul three or four nuclear submarines while it also processed two large surface ships and an aircraft carrier. Its huge capacity, along with the dozen or so smaller ship-yards throughout the country and the large Norfolk Naval Shipyard on the East Coast, was normally sufficient to keep our Navy running like a well-oiled clock.

The key words in the previous paragraph are "two large surface ships." Two large surface ships was the precise workload the Bureau of Ships in D.C. had assigned to Bremerton around the time I arrived there.

The only problem was that someone forgot to check nameplates before dispatching those particular two surface ships.

Once nuclear ships had been introduced into the Navy, the assignment of ships to overhaul yards became a more complex scheduling problem. It was no longer simply a matter of planning ship overhauls as if they were simply Chrysler 300s being assigned a repair bay. Repairing a nuclear-powered ship involved a much different workload than the same size conventionally powered surface ship.[4] And the two particular surface ships assigned to Bremerton were special indeed. They were both Lola wannabes.

In fact, *Enterprise* and *Long Beach* were close cousins of the original Lola. After *Nautilus'* original quick success, Congress, failing to recognize that the revolutionary technology change was not nuclear power but rather the marriage of nuclear power with the submarine platform (just as the technology transformation at the beginning of World War II had been the marriage of the tank with the radio), had immediately authorized building the first nuclear-powered surface ship, the cruiser *Long Beach* (CGN-9), as well as a nuclear-powered carrier, *Enterprise* (CVN-65). These two surface ships were quickly constructed, and both were commissioned in 1961, only seven years after *Nautilus* had initially rounded the New London sea buoy.

Given that the learning rate in nuclear design was extraordinarily high in those early years, the engineering plans on the first two nuclear surface ships were still a product in development. When compared with their oil-fired counterparts, these two ships would always require a greater engineering level of effort. To place these two nuclear overhauls simultaneously in the same shipyard was to dare disaster to ring the doorbell. But the Navy is such a large organization that the staffs for the surface force and the carrier force independently planned overhauls. Even worse, the respective organizations rewarded their staffs for estimating at the low end of probable costs.[5] As a result, the overhauls for *Long Beach* and *Enterprise* overlapped and were underfunded.

By the time both ships had steamed into the shipyard, the buzzards spawned from the decision for simultaneous overhaul had already begun roosting in the Bremerton trees. The people in Washington, D.C., who had scheduled the problem had long ago gone on to other roles, and—because Congress had been continually assured by many, many admirals that nuclear ships would be no more difficult than oil-fired ones to repair—there was absolutely no one in any Navy office interested in now speaking up and announcing to the world, "Whoops! We have just discovered that the first nuclear ships ever built are much more complicated (and much, much more expensive) to overhaul than the run-of-the-mill conventionally powered ship."

Within a few months after *Long Beach* and *Enterprise* had settled on their dry-dock keel blocks, so much unplanned work had originated from these two black holes that the shipyard was basically overwhelmed and unable to effectively plan. These two ships broke more items each day than the shipyard had qualified workers to repair. Since the shipyard management couldn't effectively schedule work, the shipyard workforce was working harder and getting less done.

There were other consequences. The Navy never has as many ships as it has tasks. Therefore, every day a ship of any kind is in overhaul is doubly destructive. Not only is a day in dry dock expensive; every week *Long Beach* and *Enterprise* were on keel blocks was another seven days the ships and crews at sea in the Persian Gulf and Indian Ocean were overstressed. In addition, each day an attack submarine was late getting out of overhaul (and nearly 10 percent of America's attack-submarine fleet was tied up in Puget at that time) meant another twenty-four hours a top-secret mission could not be performed or another day a ballistic-missile Soviet submarine would be free to fire nuclear missiles at the United States without the threat of being destroyed first.

One day I awoke and the tenth attack submarine was steaming up Puget Sound looking for any vacant bollard to throw a mooring line on. Do you recall that Puget had the capability to service three or four submarines? Not only was no pier available; there were insufficient qualified workers to even begin the preliminary work. Furthermore, few houses were left in Bremerton to buy, rent, or borrow, and the jobs for submarine spouses were scarce.[6] At the same time, new bars and strip joints were opening every night, and crew members had too much spare time on their hands. No one seemed terribly interested in telling Admiral Rickover (or any other senior authority) that there was a "developing situation."[7] The local people in charge were vested, like broke Grateful Dead fans, in hoping for a miracle.

I was still responsible for getting my ship, USS *Plunger* (SSN-595), out of Bremerton on schedule and under budget. With every day that went by, I feared this was less and less possible. I was also responsible for the welfare of all crew members, their wives, their children, and (it seemed) their girlfriends. The extra free time and the new bars were proving detrimental to everyone.

As I recall, the *Plunger* overhaul was initially planned to last about fourteen months, and we were off to a reasonable start until the day USS *Long Beach* appeared over the horizon. Then, weeks began passing with no appreciable progress being made on any of the major tasks involved in our overhaul.[8] I am using weeks as the unit of time measurement for two important reasons. First, I, along with all the other commanding officers, met with the shipyard admiral and his staff every week to discuss major issues in the shipyard. Second, every other week Rickover expected each nuclear commanding officer undergoing a shipyard availability to write the admiral a personal letter about the ship's progress. The letter was labeled "personal" so that it could avoid the delays in the many layers of the Navy chain of command. This personal letter went directly to Rickover's desk. Most commanding officers hated writing this missive.

From my perspective, it was an open invitation to discuss deficiencies in material, training, and personnel or whatever other problems I might think were not being adequately addressed by either me or someone in the larger Navy. I knew there was only one golden rule if I raised an issue: I had better be correct—because Rickover read each and every letter carefully. And if he thought I was in error, he would call to ensure that we "reached agreement." The call was never a social chat.

To prepare to bring the Bremerton shipyard's problems directly to the attention of Admiral Rickover, I asked my duty officers to count how many shipyard workers were actually in our spaces during each work shift. The shipyard production officer gave a presentation every Tuesday to the shipyard admiral and all the commanding officers. His brief included how many people from each of the trades (welders, shipfitters, pipefitters, etc.) were working in the back shops (on our equipment elsewhere in the shipyard) as well as the number actually working on board each ship. His numbers appeared a bit expansive to many of the submarine commanding officers.

The production officer (who was doing an excellent job in his off-hours coaching my sons in basketball) had begun providing us these data in response to continued complaints from Capt. Bill Hicks, a particularly alert fellow commander, that Hicks' submarine seemed to be deserted. Well, my compartments seemed a bit lonely too. As we were the next in line behind Hicks' submarine, I decided I should look at the same information he was reviewing. Given *Plunger*'s phase in overhaul (most machinery had been stripped from inside the hull), I had reasoned that my equipment was being worked on in the back shops scattered around the shipyard's 180 acres. But then I began listening more carefully at the Tuesday meetings.

Each week the production officer provided numbers indicating a hundred or so skilled men and women were working on board Hicks' submarine and a few less on board mine. Another couple of hundred workers (roughly evenly divided) were reportedly devoted to our equipment in the back shops. Each week Hicks missed key dates on his schedule and became more agitated. My engineer began hiking around the shipyard, visiting the inside machine shop as well as the electric motor, hydraulics, and other repair areas. He reported to me that he was unable to identify the hundred industrious souls reportedly working on our equipment. I wondered if I had misunderstood the shipyard's system.

As I was jogging one morning in the mists that tended to cling to the hills just above the waterfront, I mentally tried to integrate all this information. I decided the key had to be the time cards. The shipyard was a large organization, employing more than ten thousand people. If everyone was paid every two weeks, a system must exist to accurately record their work. If the shipyard workers weren't on board the denuded submarines, they should be documented as working elsewhere. Since the production officer said they *were* working on our equipment, then, this being the Navy, somewhere there existed records proving his case (he couldn't be lying because he was my sons' basketball coach)—and the location of those records would most likely be . . .

Now most of your friends probably avoid difficult situations. Tricky circumstances often result in someone being hurt—physically, emotionally, or professionally. Many wise people deliberately make wide detours around potential potholes in life. Of course, if you tackle problems head on and survive, they may provide a story for your grandchildren. I personally could not avoid poking at a potential problem any more than a moth can only wink appreciatively at an open flame and flutter on by.

About 2:00 a.m. the night after my jog, armed with a universal bolt cutter, a thin steel ruler, and a few other implements I had tucked into a black tool belt, I found myself sitting thoughtfully in the production officer's black leather chair, looking around as I used my right foot to swivel his seat slowly back and forth. I had carefully reclosed his front door, pulled the blinds shut, and turned on all of the lights. The building was deserted, and I hoped any outside passerby would assume the production officer was working late. I'd visited his office several times before in an attempt to try to understand why we were falling behind (he had assured me I was mistaken).

The graceful old high-ceiling wooden buildings had been built before World War II, and as I had accurately recalled, the door casings had shrunk a bit unevenly as they dried over the last hundred years. When I had inserted my steel ruler, there had been a good quarter inch between the jamb and the door lock tongue.

As I slowly rotated in his truly comfortable chair, I took in the framed pictures and models of the many fine ships built at this historical shipyard. I considered where the production officer might have filed the shop stewards' real production reports. He would never have thrown them away because the shipyard finance office needed the true reports to pay people.

But I had grown confident the shop-steward reports filed at the end of each week bore little resemblance to the weekly brief he had been providing. The row of padlocked old wooden file cabinets against the wall appeared to be taunting me. I ignored them.

Since I didn't think witnesses to the crime of breaking and entering were terribly desirable, I was alone in the production officer's office that early morning. I was sure he and I had similar survival instincts. But maybe different motives.

During my run that morning, I had come to the conclusion that he and the local admiral were under such pressure that the production officer must have begun personally altering his official reports to make it look as if work were occurring on the submarines—by skilled men and women actually assigned to work on the surface ships. My reasoning had been that he would have to keep two sets of books to maintain accurate shipyard payroll numbers, but he would never trust this duplicitous task to a subordinate who might later spill the beans. It was Monday night. He would have completed his double-bookkeeping task for tomorrow's meeting before leaving for basketball practice. I had several new locks to replace those on the safes if it came down to the universal bolt cutter.

As I continued to revolve in the production officer's chair surveying the room—I really did not want to start breaking into the safes and pawing through every folder—I noted a small pump impeller serving as a paperweight on the desk. Beneath the impeller lay a two-inch pile of single sheets of paper, face down.

Curiosity often gets a bad rap. The top sheet was a signed weekly summary report from the shipfitter shop steward for Hicks' ship. The various shipfitter skills were listed down the left side of the page with ship-hull numbers across the top; total work hours for that week were penciled in the appropriate intersecting box. There were two sections on each sheet: the top portion for work on board the ship, the bottom for back-shop work. Reports on my ship began with the eleventh sheet in the pile. I located the on-off switch for the secretary's copy machine, fired it up, and waited for what seemed like an interminable warm-up time. Some of the pencil sketches of the old sailing ships were exceptionally well done.

Later that day, after listening carefully to the production officer's brief, I sat down to write my biweekly letter to Admiral Rickover. I searched for the proper words and finally selected an opening I thought had the potential to catch his eye, "I have never met an engineering duty officer I could trust." The letter went on to request that the shipyard production officer be fired for misrepresentation.[9]

Two days later the senior submarine officer in Rickover's office, Capt. Zack Pate, called me: "Dave, Admiral Rickover received your last letter."

"Yes?"

"Do you recall that Admiral Rickover is the senior engineering duty officer in the Navy, and has been so for more than twenty years?"

I don't think Pate really expected an answer, for he continued without my reply: "He underlined your first sentence with his red pencil. He also directed the Bureau [of Personnel] to relieve the production officer at the Puget shipyard."

As you may recall, Rickover had graduated from the Naval Academy when submarines were the domain of that university's graduates. After two surface-ship tours Rickover volunteered for submarine duty and was so assigned. After his initial tour he was posted to a second submarine, in which he served as executive officer (the number-two officer on board). Unfortunately, he had been judged not sufficiently suited to be permitted to command a submarine, was reassigned back to surface-ship duty, and eventually commanded a minesweeper. Thus, in the naval service, where command at sea is the pinnacle nearly all officers strive for, Admiral Rickover had only commanded the Navy's smallest ship—a ship with limited responsibilities. A minesweeper does not project power or provide presence. It does cleanup work.

Not only had Rickover been limited in his command assignment to one of the Navy's most inconsequential ship commands; that command lasted only three months, instead of the more normal year or year and a half. By comparison, for four years I had experienced the thrill of command of USS *Plunger,* one of the most powerful ships in anyone's Navy. *Plunger* had carried the American flag unchallenged throughout the world. We had sailed alone into several oceans against America's strongest foe. My crew and I had been fortunate enough to face challenging adventures. We had received accolades and medals, and I had even gone to the White House to brief President Ronald Reagan on our ship's exploits. But *Plunger* existed because of thirty years of Rickover's dreams and work, not mine.

Yet, in my letter I had made a snide comment (inadvertent, but how would he know?). How many great men would only lightly underline in red what must have been hurtful words and then proceed to focus on the real issue—and act as I requested? Most leaders I have known could never have gotten past what they would have perceived as a personal insult. Admiral Rickover was one of life's great exceptions. He was focused only on results. He never even mentioned my letter.

However, not everything turned out for the best. My sons' athletic progress suffered. I was a terrible substitute basketball coach.

Admiral Rickover had organizationally established three independent watchdog groups in each shipyard. However, apparently not one of these groups in Bremerton felt sufficiently empowered to inform Admiral Rickover that there was proof on the hoof at the Puget Sound Naval Shipyard relevant to one of the most pressing public discussions of the day—whether nuclear surface ships required more or less repair effort than conventionally powered ships. Of course, being human, they might have been affected by Admiral Rickover's own omission of this inconvenient fact in his testimony in Congress.

This problem falls under the category of not seeing the pile of rubbish leaning against your own house. It also has to do with how a strong manager's presence can stifle disagreement. A leader can rely on one thing: If one has established a policy, promoted a specific idea, or become personally identified with a concept, no matter how many safeguards are in place to promote independent thinking, it is the rare person who will contradict a leader, no matter how absolutely wrong the chosen path.

So how does a leader or manager prevent an organization from having to rely on extraordinary corrective measures? Leadership always begins with the leader.

15

Renaissance Man

*All men are by nature conservative but conservatism in the
military profession is a source of danger to the country.*[1]

L
ife is a series of choices made, opportunities recognized or ignored, and
inequities experienced. Immediately following World War II, Admiral
Rickover seized the opportunity to develop the nuclear submarine. He
subsequently drove himself and a hand-selected team to achieve extraordinary professional success. His achievement was obviously a clear win
for him and America. Because of the palpable American fear of the Soviet
Union, Rickover remained thirty-three years in his very visible role as the
head of the naval nuclear-power program. But fear did not curtail the grow-
ing resentment. Critics, like debris pushed before a persistent wind, accumu-
lated around Admiral Rickover's feet. It was like wispy tumbleweeds slowly
being deposited against gray steps in an abandoned ghost town. When he
became less nimble, Rickover finally stumbled.[2]

It was part of life's unfairness that Admiral Rickover died before the
Cold War ended and the achievements of his nuclear submarines could be
popularized. Nevertheless, even without Rickover serving as a focal point,
over the succeeding years it became known that

- our at-sea nuclear fleet ballistic-missile submarines (sometimes carrying multiple intercontinental nuclear-tipped missiles atop each
  missile) were the survivable threat the Soviets could never hope to
  counter[3] and

- America's other nuclear underwater component, our fast-attack submarines, lurked unseen along the Soviet coasts,[4] targeting the Soviet ballistic-missile submarines, often holding the Soviet arsenal "at risk" as soon as they poked their steel noses out from the safety of their icy Soviet ports.[5]

American presidents responsible for the safety of the United States tended to appreciate being provided options other than abject capitulation or the duck-and-cover move taught in grade-school classrooms. Essentially, the men with the real need to know about the submarine fleet—the presidents of the United States—valued nuclear submarines.

Presidents also tended to notice when the safety of the United States began to deteriorate. I will provide an example that explains presidential concern. Soviet ballistic-missile subs operated from the two large Soviet submarine bases in the port cities of Vladivostok and Petropavlovsk. Periodically, Soviet submarines steamed five thousand miles east until they were in missile range of the most valuable U.S. targets.

To counter this, our attack submarines operated near Vladivostok and Petropavlovsk and endeavored to track all Soviet submarines that left these ports. This was impractical since the Soviets possessed two hundred more submarines than the United States. We therefore focused on the submarines undergoing the training for patrols off the western coast of the United States. Our secondary concerns were those submarines that might be intending operations against the Navy's battle groups. We had historically been successful, but in the late seventies the submarine-versus-submarine situation in the Pacific had been disturbed by American secrets that a group of traitors had sold to the Soviets.[6]

I do not know how the half of our submarine force in the Atlantic was doing at the time, but in the Pacific even our best U.S. skippers were having zero luck in keeping track of Soviet ballistic subs. Not surprisingly, this lack of success was a bit disconcerting to the submarine admirals— and was irritating the hell out of President Reagan. Of course, not everyone was unhappy. At least three groups were silently cheering. The first was the group of traitors at the Central Intelligence Agency (CIA) headed by Aldrich Ames and at the Navy in Norfolk (the Walker-Whitworth ring). These scoundrels had sold information to the Soviets that led to our difficulty. The second group contained a few officers wearing U.S. Air Force blue who were involved in strategic deterrence (and had felt a bit threatened by submarines since the Polaris program evolved). Those in the latter group were somewhat covert in expressing their true feelings since it was definitely not considered good form to root against fellow Americans.

The third crowd tended not to be terribly clandestine. This group comprised our fellow sailors who weren't submariners. The surface and aviation portion of the U.S. Navy annually saw 20 percent of the service's budget slide from the columns supporting aircraft and surface ships across the balance sheet to fund more and more submarines. Aviators and surface officers had grown to view submarines as useless for "real wars" like Vietnam. These officers were also professionally a bit irritated because physics dictated that airplanes and surface ships had little capability against submarines. Fanning these ill feelings was the policy that submarine missions were too sensitive for anyone other than a few submariners to know about.[7] This policy had successfully established a secure environment for information and also a nearly perfect breeding ground for resentment. The submarine force was generally despised throughout the Navy. As a consequence, several groups hoped that a loss of presidential confidence in submarines would soon result in fewer submarines being authorized by Congress. As one might suspect, the tension in the Pacific was nearly tangible.

At the time I commanded USS *Plunger*, one of the oldest attack submarines in the fleet. We were as fast as newer submarines, but our living spaces were more Spartan and our equipment less reliable. However, our sensor and analysis equipment had been continually updated over the years and was nearly as good as that on the newest ship. On the positive side, we had just returned from a successful thirteen-month overseas deployment, meaning our crew was well trained and experienced.

This recent deployed experience (and our availability when other ships were not) more than balanced any concern about equipment deficiencies, so when intelligence was received that the Soviets had a ballistic-missile submarine out and about, the job of turning the five-year detection drought around fell to *Plunger*. Our task was to locate the Soviet sub and determine what tactics she was using to make her way undetected back and forth across the Pacific. Reducing a several-month story to its essence, we were successful.[8]

After we had returned, it was in the best interests of the submarine force to make a grand example of *Plunger*'s accomplishment (this would serve to assail doubters, both foreign and domestic). I was thus instructed to put together a briefing for President Reagan. A fellow skipper, Hank Chiles,[9] had also just completed an excellent patrol, and although he would not be briefing the president, Chiles and I together gave our briefs to a great of number of interested Washington, D.C., offices.

As we were so doing, we learned that Admiral Rickover had heard that Chiles and I were going to be in Washington, D.C., and wanted to hear our briefs. We both had time in our schedule. We had just been over to see Rich Haver, who had been the Navy's expert on the Soviets for nearly as long as there had been submarines (to be completely fair, he is younger than I), and our briefs had ended early. Both Chiles and I suspected our briefings were also a form of personal interview, as the word on the street was that Rickover was looking for a new special assistant, a job both of us desired. The role had proved to be a sure path for promotion to the rank of admiral (Chiles was probably never that shallow, but I was).

We briefed the admiral and his staff in a little room packed with men sitting on armless chairs. Watching his eyes as I spoke, I remember thinking that the admiral was eighty and still absorbing everything I said. I also remember the intake of breath when I mentioned that (at one time in the thirteen-month deployment) I was playing a pickup game of basketball in Guam when a messenger brought me word that *Plunger* was needed off Thailand. Less than three hours later, our submarine was submerged and headed south-southwest at flank speed. (I had thrown this little bon mot into the brief to emphasize the readiness of our engineering plant, even when we were a year overdue for a planned overhaul.)

"You were doing what?" Instead of smiling his approval, the admiral was glaring at me. Off to my right I heard Chiles softly chortling.

"Flank." (This is the Navy term for the fastest ship speed.)

"No, before that."

I unsuccessfully racked my brain.

Finally, ratcheting his face up into its most menacing glare, Rickover took pity on my inability to recall: "Why were you playing some sport instead of studying or reading? That might improve your mind!"

Oops! I had forgotten that it was "nuclear lore" that the admiral derided anyone who participated in sports. I had always assumed his derision was not actually serious but for his own amusement. As it so happened, I had my own sports fiction ongoing with my two sons, so I straightened myself up to my full five-foot-ten-inch height: "I need to stay in shape, Admiral. When I retire from your program, I promised my two sons that I am going to earn money by playing in the National Basketball Association."

Quickly, before he could decide to engage in a contest of wits and destroy me, I shifted to a backup slide that the director of naval intelligence had told me to remove from the presentation intended for the White House the following day. "Admiral, if I had stayed in my room in Guam, I would only have been more worried about this particular piece of information we gathered. A lot of people believe it is extraneous. I am not so sure. I haven't been able to figure out what it means. It's something new. No one in any of the eleven groups that Hank and I have briefed over the last few weeks has been able to offer any supposition as to what the Soviets are doing."

If the room was quiet after our sports repartee, it was now completely silent. The slight hum of the projector fan sounded like the rush of water over Niagara Falls—just before someone drops to his death in a barrel. The admiral's eyes narrowed as he skimmed over the slide, taking in the information USS *Plunger* had acquired at some risk. After a few seconds his shoulders relaxed, and he slightly sighed, almost under his breath.

I have often since wondered whether or not it was the exhale of a man who had sometimes in the dark of night wished he had been better able to push himself beyond his introverted personality. I was watching every movement of his pupils as they darted about the slide and then focused on one particular sketch I had made of what I had seen. After a few seconds he rose from his seat, took my pointer, and walked over to the screen.

He turned and spoke across the audience to me, even though it was evident he was performing for his staff: "This should be obvious. The Soviets are . . ." He then related the conclusion he had drawn from the information I had presented, explaining to us all what was then immediately clear to his small audience (and which remains to this day classified information). His conclusions made several other previously uncorrelated observations quickly mate and lock in my mind. A few seconds later he handed back my pointer and exited the room without a word.

I inserted the former backup slide into the primary brief for the White House and the next day used the admiral's explanation in my presentation to the president's staff without shame, as if it were my own. I also mentally added the admiral's superior knowledge of Soviet navy tactics to the list of talents I already had recognized. Still, Rickover selected Hank Chiles to be his next special assistant.

Chiles' selection is worth a special comment, for never for a second did I think Admiral Rickover selected him because of my inadvertent sports remark (although when Chiles and I ate dinner that night, we both agreed I must have been brain-dead to tempt the admiral with my Guam basketball remark). The admiral often made disparaging comments to determine if a person could think on his feet and had the personal gumption to respond to Rickover's challenges.

In this particular situation I have a good case to disprove all of those who believe they were not accepted into the nuclear program because they were exceptional athletes (you can find their stories littering the Internet). Chiles had actually been an All-American athlete at the Naval Academy, but I have a far stronger proof.

When I returned from the briefings in D.C., USS *Plunger* and I sailed immediately to Bremerton, Washington, where we entered the Puget Sound Naval Shipyard. The professional pressure in Bremerton was much less than on board an operating ship, and during the overhaul I had time to coach my sons in soccer and basketball. Now, while I have played quite a bit of basketball (I was born in Indianapolis, where the desire to dribble is injected into the placenta while the mother is giving birth in Methodist Hospital), I had never participated in soccer. Therefore, to learn how to play in order to teach my young sons, I had joined a local semipro soccer team. How hard could this sport be? I said to myself. It was certainly not tackle football.

At the time I was thirty-nine years old. I had spent twenty-six of the previous twenty-eight months at sea and thirty of the last forty months away from home—and I was perhaps not in the best of shape. Perhaps I was feeling a little guilty about my absence during such critical years for my sons. I may have underestimated the contact involved in soccer. I acknowledge never being great about knowing my limits. In our first game my nose was crushed, my right eye orbit was broken, and sufficient blood vessels were ruptured in my brain to result in a subdural hematoma. I was flown by helicopter to a hospital to remove half my skull to relieve pressure on my brain.

As soon as I was out of surgery, my operational commander called me in the hospital and told my wife, "Tell Dave not to worry about anything, we just won't tell Admiral Rickover."

The "anything" to which he was referring was that everyone assumed Rickover would press to have me immediately removed from command. This wasn't simply a broken leg. I wasn't even going to be able to visit the ship for months. We were in dry dock, but Rickover insisted that someone always be responsible. It was nice of my boss to think he was protecting me, but "We won't tell Admiral Rickover"? Hello!

I was in a hospital bed and covered with wires. I couldn't move and had a breathing tube down my throat. However, nothing was blocking my thinking process. So I lay there and considered the likelihood of my operational commander's statement proving to be accurate. A shipyard is a bit similar to a town of 15,000 to 20,000 people—except that people live a lot closer together and gossip more in a shipyard. Admiral Rickover had three teams in the Puget shipyard that independently reported to him what was happening on those acres. Was it likely that the three teams could be sworn to silence? I mentally reviewed them.

The first was my boss in the shipyard (in the military one often has more than one senior to whom he or she is responsible). He was a former nuclear-submarine commanding officer and, along with a small staff, had been assigned to the shipyard to provide advice and counsel to the commanding officers there. The particular officer in Puget was the legendary

Dave Minton of USS *Guardfish* fame, and he, along with his wonder-ful wife, Marilyn, and their daughter, Davie, were great friends of ours.[10] However, Dave was a true professional, and professionalism trumps friend-ship in the nuclear business seven days of every week. I was sure Dave would put his own evaluation of the state of my physical and mental recov-ery in each and every one of his biweekly letters to Rickover.

The second person in the Puget Sound area who wrote a biweekly letter to Admiral Rickover was a senior civilian who had worked for the admiral for twenty years, periodically moving among the various nuclear shipyards. This individual filled the role of the Naval Reactors shipyard representative and managed a small group of technicians tasked to ensure everyone in the shipyard was following all the details involved in the myr-iad processes entailed by nuclear power. The nuclear-power world is small, and the wife of this senior civilian actually had attended high school one desert town over from the farm my wife grew up on.

As a result, I knew that the Naval Reactors shipyard representa-tive's spouse had met her husband while she was performing in one of the strip clubs that filled a notorious block in the one-Idaho-town-over. This unimportant but titillating fact had become clear a decade earlier, dur-ing an admiral's garden party, when, in casual conversation, after finding they were from the same low-density areas, my wife had asked the Naval Reactors representative's spouse, "What clubs did you belong to?" For a minute the woman must have thought she had found a true kindred spirit from back home. My wife had meant high school clubs, like 4-H and Tri-Hi-Y, but that was not what was heard. During the moment of silence that always seems to mysteriously descend for these truly inappropriate cocktail party lines, the other woman's clear voice rang out, "The Silver Spur, The Naked Chaps . . ."

Her husband and I never bonded. Somehow, I felt he might see it as his responsibility to mention that I was even less attentive than usual to my ship duties.

The third biweekly Rickover letter writer was the admiral who ran Puget shipyard. This was the same man who had recently reluctantly fired his best friend for falsifying time cards. Five weeks had passed. I wondered if he still remembered. His grand house lay immediately behind ours on the naval base, separated by only a grassy swale the neighborhood children used for sports. The previous week, while playing baseball, one of my sons had broken the glass in the admiral's back door.

Admiral Rickover wouldn't know about my state—fat chance!

It took a few months for my hair to grow back in where my skin had been grafted. It was another few months before my gait was completely steady. Yet Rickover never did call me to tell me how dumb it was to play a sport (at the semipro level when I didn't even know all the rules).[11] I later learned he did telephone my boss's boss. He instructed him to call my executive officer every day—to see if my number two needed anything in the way of assistance until I was fully healed and back at work—and not to inform me. I didn't hear from, see, or speak to Adm. Hyman G. Rickover again.

One hot July morning a few years later, I reflectively donned the white uniform bearing my own admiral's gold shoulder boards and joined the thousand other quiet mourners for the admiral's service within the heavy cool gray stones of the Washington National Cathedral.

Admiral Rickover only periodically received intelligence briefings on Soviet navy operations, yet he was able to quickly discern a new concept the Soviets were in the process of adopting (time later validated Rickover's hypothesis). The remainder of the submarine and intelligence communities (and me, of course, who actually witnessed the events on site) had failed to identify the patterns Rickover instantly recognized. Does this incident indicate anything about the flexibility of Admiral Rickover's mind? Can you capture this imagination in an organization? How?

Do you think Admiral Rickover was particularly loyal to those people he considered his top performers? Are you? Is this good for the organization? What are the possible problems with a nuanced, as opposed to consistent, approach to all your managers?

16

Innovation and Change

*Sit down before fact with an open mind. Be prepared to
give up every preconceived notion. . . . Don't push out figures
when facts are going in the opposite direction.*[1]

I have waited some years after Admiral Rickover's death to write this book.
The practical reason was that I was employed in a job that left little time
for reflective writing. I also thought the passage of time might help me
approach the subject with refreshed insight.

During the years after his passing, I worked with hundreds of
senior leaders who advocated a number of different management styles.
Following Rickover's memorial service, I sequentially held three jobs
within the Navy not associated with the submarine force. After retiring
from the Navy, I spent another two decades in work divorced from the
Navy—as a director on various public company boards, in executive roles
with two major companies, and, in succession, as a political appointee in
the Clinton administration, as an owner of a small business, as the senior
adviser to the minister of finance in Iraq, and then back to business as
the chief operating officer of a large organization performing both defense
and commercial work.

In each of these roles, I drew on the lessons I had learned from my personal interactions with Admiral Rickover. Each time circumstances tested
me, I became even more convinced that the admiral's leadership and management techniques could aid any manager. His principles were out there
for all to see but tended to become lost in the amazing story of his career.[2]
I finally realized that residual resentment in the Navy and defense industry

revolved around the cultural changes he forced. This situation was not helped when the good admiral, himself an expert at distinguishing pearls from dross, was too busy after he had finally retired to ever get around to writing his own autobiography.

But, second only to the establishment of the nuclear-submarine force,[3] Rickover's most important achievements were the management innovations he gave the world. My personal interactions with him led me to three observations:

- Hard work and focus can succeed for anyone,
- Humans can manage process control as well as continuous change at the same time, and
- An extraordinary leader can see well "beyond the horizon."

Hard Work

I never met anyone who worked harder than Rickover. No one. And he was a member of a tough crowd, for unlike some leaders, Rickover did not surround himself with lesser intellects and personalities. Instead, he preferentially selected younger Type A personalities and let it be known that he valued and rewarded dedication. Still, no one I met ever outworked him.

I think he remained driven because this characteristic was what best discriminated him from his peers. Rickover's early professional life did not show the same signs of brilliance we have grown to expect to see in young people who will change the world. Yet, after a slow twenty-five-year professional start, Rickover altered everything he touched.

He had two personal characteristics working mightily against him: his introversion and his lack of command presence. It is difficult to determine the more limiting trait, but let's take the introvert issue first. His dislike of social engagements he couldn't control led him to be classified as a loner by his peers. It also limited his effectiveness. Management (and leadership) is made effective by using others' hands and minds to enhance and accomplish one's own vision. Rickover permitted his natural shyness to constrain his ability to establish political and professional alliances. Consequently, he was unsuccessful in some of his endeavors, and other achievements required more effort than they might have.

Being an introvert is a perfectly acceptable trait in many career fields, but by choosing to attend the Naval Academy, Rickover had become part of a profession in which introversion was a handicap. Naval officers were expected to share bonhomie with others from all cultures and walks of life. An officer needed to develop relationships with military officers and government officials from other nations. The Navy anticipated that as an officer progressed through different jobs and grew more senior, those cold-call friendships could lead to informal or formal alliances for the good of the United States.

The Navy officer corps has historically been an important adjunct to the U.S. ambassadorial effort. For example, during Rickover's attendance at the U.S. Naval Academy, sons of important individuals from each ally also attended. After graduation these young individuals returned to their home countries to serve as officers and political officials. Given the millions of dollars our government invested in establishing the framework for development of these high-level contacts, junior officers were expected (and graded upon) their ability to continue to build on these relationships. Rickover refused to make any attempt to do so and ridiculed those officers who did.

Since Rickover was by nature profoundly uncomfortable in social settings and with most personal relationships, it was painful to be in his presence.[4] This was not itself a fatal flaw, but management is always accomplished by working with people, and when staff members are uncomfortable, less gets done. The admiral appears never to have been sufficiently at ease and confident to experiment with altering his management and leadership style. He thus had difficulty getting more from the less-capable individuals who make up the bulk of every organization. Rickover worked well with the supremely confident, brash, intelligent, articulate, and outspoken personalities he sought to recruit. But those numbers are always limited (thank goodness). As the nuclear-submarine force grew, Rickover needed more people, and many of those, although very bright, were not completely comfortable with Rickover's "in your face" approach. While the nuclear-submarine force needed all these personnel, Rickover often did not relate as well to the "purer souls" as he did to the "aggressive bastards."

For all of his accomplishments, there is no evidence that Rickover sought to alter his personal management style to accommodate the wide range of personalities working for him. A reading of the accounts of his own time on board submarines (where the extremely small size of submarine crews makes the growth of interactive people skills imperative) indicates that Rickover's undeveloped personal skills marred the experience for him as well as for his shipmates.[5]

As he rose in seniority within the Navy, his introversion may have been part of his larger challenge with command presence. No one has ever been able to explain why one particular individual is considered to have command presence while another is found wanting. Perhaps it is just the way one holds one's mouth. If so, Rickover did not hold his the right way. In reviewing the literature and oral histories of his peers, as well as speaking to those who worked for or with him, I have found few, whether or not they admired Rickover, who thought the admiral had the intangible presence and bearing of a leader. He was without peer as a manager, but the leadership mantle tended to slip from his thin shoulders. I always believed this was personally devastating to him. Rickover wanted to be known as a leader, not as the most superlative manager of his century.[6]

It is similarly difficult to tell what caused him the most anguish during his command tour in his thirties on board the minesweeper USS *Finch*, another small, intimate ship.[7] Nevertheless, a short time after he had arrived in *Finch* to assume command, Rickover left the role naval officers are culturally predisposed to savor above all others—command at sea—to become an engineering duty officer, no longer eligible to command anything at sea. It was a good decision given that he wanted to continue a career in the Navy, for many naval officers did not believe command presence was essential in the engineering-only field.

Although his engineering expertise was respected, Rickover was never ordered into the war zones during the nearly five years of World War II[8] but was instead sent to Oak Ridge, Tennessee, at the war's completion, in charge of literally no one.[9] It is normally a professional disaster for a captain in the Navy to have no staff.

At the time he arrived at the hastily constructed wooden buildings that were Oak Ridge, Captain Rickover was nearly fifty years old. During his career he had not been shot at in battle, he had not been successful in operations at sea, and he had not been successful in senior billets at sea. Already there were admirals serving in the Pacific who had graduated from the Naval Academy later than he. Yet a short eight years later (January 11, 1954), the entire cover of *Time* magazine would be devoted to Captain Rickover's stern visage.

At Oak Ridge Rickover did not suddenly become a new man. He was not immediately different from what he had been for the first half of his life. Instead, he found himself assigned to a situation that, to use a baseball expression, was in his personal capabilities' "sweet spot." Like the immortal Lou Gehrig, given a chance at bat, Hyman G. Rickover hit it out of the ballpark—and continued doing so for more than three decades.

While others initially yearned to be in charge of the Navy's nuclear effort, none were able or willing to devote their life and health solely to this one goal. Fitting the first nuclear reactor in the world into the small round hull of a submarine demanded a manager with the ability to understand both science and engineering. The manager needed not only to observe process guidelines but also to simultaneously innovate—and possess more than a handful of chutzpah.

The final hurdle Rickover leaped—another his peers couldn't match—was that he possessed the energy required. Rickover had spent his entire life working at an extraordinary pace. Others had permitted their life to become distracted by such things as families, church, and recreation. Rickover had never diverted his focus from work. The right problem at Oak Ridge had found the right man.

Process versus Innovation

Most successful organizations attribute their triumphs to the good processes they have instituted and inculcated. Processes are the tools that enable inexperienced and less-capable employees to fight well above their weight. Repeatable processes allow an organization to retain lessons learned.

Admiral Rickover insisted that the nuclear-submarine force become the advocate within the Navy for strict process control. Not only did the majority of the Navy not follow his lead, but some surface officers led a countermovement. The counterweapon of choice was to ridicule submariners as unthinking robots (i.e., surface officers did not need processes because they thought through their problems rather than relying on authoritarian guidance). This was a powerful emotional argument. Its flaws were often not understood, especially by individuals not terribly interested in engineering knowledge becoming construed as essential to naval professionalism. Submariners were thus pushed by their officer peers, as well as many public figures, to denigrate and ignore Rickover's standards. Peer pressure is a strong weapon in enforcing conformity.

But Rickover was mentally tougher than the sum of his critics. By sheer force of personality, he refused to permit his small group of submariners to relax their standards (and goodness knows we all had weak moments when it seemed easier to join rather than fight the much larger group of officers who were our social friends and peers). However, Rickover was adamant about his standards and dismissed anyone who showed weakness. At the same time, he was more willing than anyone I have ever known to adopt new ideas and change if a hitherto approved process were subsequently demonstrated incorrect. It did not matter to him if he had personally conceived the idea that was being dragged through the mud and ridiculed. Rickover lived his life by the measures he had publicly listed during his U.S. Naval Postgraduate School address in 1954, and one of those was that rules limit progress.[10]

By insisting on strict process control for routine evolutions yet concurrently encouraging individuals to challenge his system and his processes, Rickover was able to institute a scheme in which individuals did not have to choose between process and innovation.[11] The nuclear-submarine force would value both.

Beyond the Horizon

His other demonstrated talents aside, I have personally always been in awe of how Admiral Rickover could see so clearly far into the future. He initially demonstrated this valuable talent during his assignment to Oak Ridge in the late forties. His different biographers speak of all the various tactical actions Rickover undertook in order for the program to succeed (and for his own professional aspirations to thrive). In this early process he made three immensely important strategic decisions:

- He decided to gain simultaneous control of the AEC or Department of Energy aspects of their maritime program and the Navy nuclear program.
- He decided, counter to the recommendations of his entire team, to increase the radiation shielding (and lower the radiation exposure of the crew).
- He decided the first nuclear reactor in the world would go into the immensely more confined spaces of a submarine instead of the planned (and much more engineering-friendly) surface ship.

I have previously discussed the critical importance to America of the first two decisions. To recap, gaining control of both the AEC and the Navy nuclear program by hook or crook prevented bureaucratic sluggishness when the United States and the Soviet Union were engaged in the Cold War. At the same time, establishing low radiation limits may well have been one of the key factors in the outcome of the Cold War.

Rickover's insistence on placing the first reactor on board a submarine (instead of a surface ship) hasn't been discussed in this book simply because I was not present, as others were, when Rickover reversed the Navy's decision to go with a surface ship as the pilot project platform—and consequently changed history.[12] Rickover understood, while many did not, that blending essential submarine characteristics with a nuclear power plant was as revolutionary a change as if, after having landed their World War I German Fokker propeller-driven biplanes, U.S. airmen had walked directly across the beaten-down grass of a French meadow, handed their leather helmets to a beautiful mademoiselle, and climbed up a steel ladder directly into the cockpits of Stealth F-117 Nighthawks. I cannot even conjure a ground-force analogy, unless it would be as if a warrior on the front lines facing an enemy had passed a broken medieval bow and quiver of arrows back over his shoulder and received in return a Spencer repeating rifle.

The diesel submarine had previously been among the least-capable ships in the naval fleet, most useful as a scout or for hit-and-run tactics against merchant ships.[13] By putting nuclear power on board submarines, Rickover truly transformed the U.S. Navy and altered the balance of naval warfare between the two superpowers.

Consolidating bureaucratic control of the nuclear-power program, strictly limiting the radiation exposure of the crews, and deciding the first reactor would go on board a submarine were important, but Rickover also made three other key decisions that bundled together comprise his personal "crystal-ball six-pack":

- Long before there was any public outcry to do so, Rickover decreed that nuclear vessels would not permit any radioactive contamination to be released into the environment.
- He decided that the culture of the submarine force would emphasize engineering competency as a priority over any other skill.[14]
- He focused on safety, safety, safety.

Release of Radioactivity

Those who live in an environment of mature and regulated industries often do not appreciate how new technologies begin. It is difficult to later go back and reproduce the conditions at the creation, when enthusiasm was high and before (often subtle) dangers were fully recognized or appreciated. Often, when a new technology is initially being exploited, the perceived threat of failure mitigates a proper appreciation of the risks.

When I began serving in submarines, our standard process permitted discharging primary coolant, the water that flowed through the reactor and gathered radioactive corrosion by-products during its journey, directly out of the ship (in my particular case into the Thames River in New London) on outgoing tides. Once off the ship the coolant was theoretically diluted to a harmless mixture by all the other water and swept past the boots of the early rising men fishing from the Groton pier butts into Narragansett Bay. Discharging radioactive coolant overboard seemed to me like a necessary and natural practice. I didn't question it, nor do I recall anyone having second thoughts at the time. Doing so was even a technical necessity, for the ships couldn't start up without discharging coolant. There was simply no place to put the excess water when the reactor primary plant was heated up several hundreds of degrees. In addition, many of the systems supporting reactor operation were designed to leak.

Remember that Rickover only had control of the systems immediately supporting reactor operation. The myriad other support systems were designed and built by the Bureau of Ships (which was never under Rickover's control, no matter how much he desired it to be). Rather than devote the effort to designing original valves for this new underwater application, the bureau often adapted previously designed valves intended for high-pressure surface-ship steam engineering plant applications. As a consequence, these valves typically relied on a small leakage of water from the inside, past the stem,[15] to ease the friction of the valve opening and closing.[16] But when these valves were installed in nuclear submarines, the lubricating water leaking by the stem of each valve contained a small amount of radioactive fission products. Because of this design, on the first several classes of nuclear ships, a constant trickle of contaminated water dripped into submarine bilges.[17] Not only were the bilges being contaminated in the process, but as natural evaporation occurred, a small amount of radioactive particles became airborne.

It wasn't that much radiation, and those of us serving in the older nuclear submarines had become accustomed to it. Rickover, however, recognized the situation for the real danger it posed—if not to sailors, to principle. Whether large or small, the trickle of water was uncontrolled and caused unnecessary radiation exposure. Rickover had a simple standard: radioactivity was either under control or not. It did not matter whether the radioactivity released was significant. But it mattered a great deal that the leakage was a violation of his principle of controlling unnecessary exposure to humans.[18]

And while he was at it, Rickover worried about the general public and the unanticipated dangers that might result from the water discharged overboard. In the early seventies he surprised me—and, I think, most of us who were operating his ships—by, without warning, simply dictating that we would no longer discharge any radioactive liquids into the sea. It did not matter that submarines had been designed in a matter that required pumping radioactive waste overboard. He did not care about past mistakes or the more than fifteen years that the submarine Navy had been discharging contamination overboard without ill results. He was not moved by claims of constancy. He was not swayed by professional embarrassment. Rickover had come to the conclusion that the old practice was wrong. We who were operating the ships were not given a new solution. We were only made responsible for determining how to forever cease discharging radioactivity overboard.[19]

Smart people thought and adapted. The first systems were labor and supervisory intensive. Later, more elegant designs replaced our first rough efforts. Some nuclear operators did not adapt or accept how important

Rickover thought this change. Those individuals were, by definition, less flexible than safety required, and they were replaced with people with greater imagination, initiative, and drive.

Years later it became evident that "the organizational we" had greatly underestimated the danger of the insidious buildup over time of radioactive contaminants in the seabeds adjacent to our common ships' moorings. By the time the facts were in, because Rickover had taken early action, the danger was already decaying away. Rickover had not spent years agonizing about the consequences of a change in policy. He had not had numerous teams analyze the data. He did not worry about the cost of change (or spend hours listening to lawyers harp about the possible costs of consequential lawsuits). He simply trusted his gut and changed. By doing so, he stopped the submarine force from discharging radioactivity into the environment long before the issue ever crystallized in the public eye. We stopped solely because Admiral Rickover could perceive the inherent principles and see where the facts would eventually lead a reasonable person (or at least one with the admiral's insight).

Submarine-Culture Change

From his own experience as a younger officer, Rickover knew that the Navy had an inordinate respect for the admirals who had served in command at sea.[20] These admirals ultimately controlled the Navy. Since they had been selected in part because they possessed command presence, they believed in the importance of that characteristic.

The same power structure valued command at sea above all other achievements. Consequently, Navy culture denigrated engineering. The officers in the seagoing Navy who rose to admiral rank had seldom served as engineers. Gunnery was the common path to flag rank. And people on the way to flag rank believed they did not have the time to serve as engineers. Like most of us, they also frequently did not have the inclination. Rickover recognized that the existing Navy power structure would never value the engineering knowledge he believed was essential. He could either change the culture of the Navy's entire power structure—one that had managed to last for two hundred years—or he could do something more innovative. Since the first was impossible, even for Rickover, he selected the latter.

He chose to assemble a corps of men who were mentally agile enough to assimilate nuclear engineering during their first eight to ten years. At the same time, he recruited driven men who he judged would be willing to spend the second ten to fifteen years of their careers working extra hard to successfully compete as conventional "operating" admirals.[21] Rickover managed this, not by recruiting individuals like him to follow in his own footsteps, but by choosing individuals who could be more than he. The men who had judged Rickover's early career had driven home to him that he could not be a successful warrior—the most respected label in the Navy—but was "only" qualified to be an engineering manager. Rickover knew he needed men within the operating Navy who understood the principles of nuclear safety as well as he—and who were in positions of power. Those positions are filled with admirals.

So, he selected men for nuclear power who had the innate ability to be warriors and leaders. To establish the culture of engineering excellence he needed, he insisted that every officer who aspired to command a nuclear submarine first qualify as an engineer (and for many years every nuclear-submarine officer selected to be promoted to admiral had previously served as an engineer). By ignoring conventional wisdom and establishing a new pecking order, Rickover thus subordinated the navigations, operations, and weapons officers assignments to the individual assigned as engineer (the Navy previously allotted much higher status to these billets than to the engineer assignment). And then Rickover stayed in place in the Navy to ensure that his new culture of engineering management would flourish. He thus established a completely unique and different subculture within the naval culture.

Safety, Safety, Safety

It is important to review the impact Rickover had on the concept of safety. Going to sea in submarines is inherently dangerous. Nuclear power also has its dangers. Yet the United States has not lost a submarine since the 1960s, and America has never had a reactor accident, while our peer competitor in this area, the Soviet Union/Russia, has both lost submarines and suffered many reactor accidents.

Why the differences? Is it because Russia produces fewer scientists than America? No, Russia produces more scientists in absolute numbers as well as in college percentages. So the difference is not education. I can personally assure you it is also not talent. The Soviets have directed some of their finest young men to their submarine programs, and these men have served with distinction, performing many brave and selfless acts.[22] The difference between the two countries was and remains one of culture.[23]

Rickover recognized that safety was the most important aspect of the U.S. Navy's nuclear power program. He installed principles to ensure all nuclear-trained Americans recognized their personal responsibility to protect the public from any adverse effects of nuclear power. He then devoted the rest of his life to ensuring this cultural change was embedded into the nuclear-submarine force.

17

A Culture of Adaptation

To doubt one's own first principles is the mark of a civilized man. Don't defend past actions; what is right today may be wrong tomorrow. Don't be consistent; consistency is the refuge of fools.[1]

n July 1986, four years after he had been forced to retire, Admiral Rickover died. It is useful to recall that on the day he passed, whereas the Vietnam War (1959–75) was thankfully over, the Cold War and the accompanying arms race with the Soviet Union still showed no signs of abatement. Few diesel submarines remained in the U.S. Navy inventory.[2] Yet nearly a third of active Navy ships were nuclear submarines.[3] Of the remaining fleet, a half dozen of the cruisers and destroyers were also nuclear powered, as was every aircraft carrier built since Robert McNamara had been secretary of defense. Women were filling critical roles on board nearly every ship in the Navy except submarines.[4]

In the Navy the leadership at Naval Reactors had been successfully passed to Kin McKee (who had still never addressed the *Nautilus* main seawater valves) without apparent discontinuities. Rickover had used his three decades at the Naval Reactors helm to put his personal imprint on the officers who served throughout the nuclear-power program. Those who followed him were true believers. In the years Rickover ran Naval Reactors, he had personally interviewed each officer candidate—personally approved their training—and personally approved the credentials of each person who served as an engineer or commanding officer. He had read thousands of letters from commanding officers who periodically wrote to him and had individually spoken to thirty years of commanders by telephone if they displeased

him. Less frequently, he also called if he thought a performance deserved special praise. Each of his senior officers knew him and his voice even if they
recognized no other admiral in the Navy. Almost all of the three thousand
officers in the submarine force, including me, believed they knew him.[5]

By the time Rickover was forced to retire, he had firmly established
an enduring culture of "just do what is right." That culture would guide
the easing of the rudder a bit when it became evident the Kindly Old
Gentleman had initially advocated the wrong course or when the heading
of the submarine force needed to adapt to changing weather conditions,
such as the unexpected end of the Cold War. One measure of the strength
of the culture Admiral Rickover established is the ease with which significant changes were made after his death. I am sure there were many such
changes. I was personally involved in three.

Bringing the Rudder Over: Decommissioning the Nuclear Surface Ships

The first course correction involved unraveling one of the programs that
Rickover had firmly supported (if the program had been successful, it
would have made both submarine and commercial nuclear power less
expensive in the United States).

From 1988 to 1990 I was an admiral on the West Coast, responsible
for training the attack submarines there and, as military officers are often
fond of primly stating, "other duties as assigned." One of those assigned
duties was responsibility for the annual safety drills of the nuclear surface
ships on the West Coast; I was the flag officer responsible for checking the
nuclear safety of ships, yet another admiral had all other responsibilities
for those same ships. This cockamamie arrangement had become necessary
because the surface force had not routinely selected nuclear officers for flag
rank. As a result of the surface community's failure to promote sufficient
qualified officers to look after the safety aspects of their ships,[6] that specific
responsibility had been assigned to the senior submariner in the local area.

So, during my day job I was responsible for everything on board my
own sixty submarines (as well as the forty surface ships supporting them)
and could reassign priorities, money, people, and assets as I saw necessary
to accomplish my mission. I was held completely responsible—my reputation, my career, and my freedom at risk—for all the results. I had willingly
accepted that unspoken contract when I had donned the broad gold uniform stripe that designates an individual as an admiral.

When I walked on board nuclear surface ships, it was as if I entered a
different world. I well remembered a similar culture from my diesel-boat

days. Surface ships outside the propulsion spaces retained the culture of diesel boats. Attention was on operations. The engineering plant was expected to get by. This was obviously an unsatisfactory situation.

One might change the culture of the surface force, but all attempts thus far had been unsuccessful. With the visible success of nuclear submarines (and the constant harping of Admiral Rickover), senior officers had led several efforts to change the approach of surface sailors toward engineering. All had failed. But given the opportunity, people do not behave completely irrationally. Why did the surface force essentially ignore the engineering plant? For the best of all possible reasons: surface ships weren't submarines.

A surface ship did not provide presence simply by getting under way. A surface ship needed to have radars activated and guns or missiles visibly ready. In addition, when submerged a submarine is nearly invulnerable, susceptible to attack only in special circumstances. A surface ship could not become nearly invulnerable by simply slipping below the waves. It was potentially targetable 24/7. My experience is that the submarine commanding officer can often control the level of risk by choosing when to close (or, alternatively, open) dangerous situations. On board a surface ship, the environment chooses you. Finally, if a surface ship's engineering plant stops, no one immediately dies (as might occur on board a submerged submarine). A surface ship simply floats until it is joined by one of its sister ships and can be towed or repaired. Given all the differences, is it surprising that surface-ship officers choose to pay the most attention to what is keeping them alive and maximize their warfighting capability?

Of course, this logic did not solve the nuclear safety concerns. Just as two dissimilar biological cultures will not usually exist in the same petri dish, it is difficult to maintain two separate cultures on board one ship. Rickover had destroyed the diesel culture in the submarine force because he knew the diesel-boat environment did not fit with highly technical operations like nuclear power (and the diesel boat was actually a surface ship, while the nuclear variant was the first true submarine). As I visited the nuclear surface ships, I believed I could easily predict the culture that would eventually prevail on board surface ships now that Rickover was gone.

If you are a student of Navy history, you will know that Rickover pushed hard for many years for an all-nuclear Navy. He thought that having every ship powered by nuclear power would relieve the Navy from the tyranny of the price of oil. He also insisted that nuclear power would release the Navy from relying on a network of support bases (primarily for oil resupply) and that unarmed oilers were vulnerable ships during wartime. By giving public speeches and using his influence in Congress, Rickover had succeeded in getting nuclear power on aircraft carriers as well as seven cruisers. However, his argument of increased mobility, flexibility, and warfighting agility had in the end failed to carry the day for surface ships other than carriers.

I carefully followed this public discussion during the sixties and seventies. The opposing argument for nonnuclear ships (what Admiral Zumwalt had advocated and termed the *high-low mix*) was that the construction cost of the nonnuclear ships was much, much less than that of nuclear ships. Thus, for the same amount of up-front money, one could have more surface ships, and those ships obviously could be in more places—always a concern when three-quarters of the globe is water.

In addition, the Navy would always need oilers and their infrastructure for transport aviation gas and munitions, as well as food and spare parts, from shore to the carriers for the aircraft flying from the big decks (refueling the destroyers is a minor additional burden). Examining the issue revealed that even if one achieved an all-nuclear surface-ship fleet, oilers, resupply ships, and the supporting infrastructure (fuel farms, tanks, etc.) located around the world would still be necessary. In addition, as both sides carefully avoided noting, the operation of a nuclear plant requires a person with much higher training.

I thought it was noteworthy that no one ever discussed the key training differentiator. Good people are always harder to find than money. Did no one recall the trouble Rickover had in locating sufficient people to run 150 submarines (each surface ship had a much larger wardroom than any submarine)? As I followed the public argument over the years, I couldn't fathom how we would ever find enough qualified people to operate the six hundred ships we were trying to put to sea at the time if they were all nuclear-powered.

I had been leaning toward the side of Rickover's opponents for some years. The physics seemed fairly simple: there was air on the surface and none below the water. This led to an obvious conclusion: nuclear power was essential to submarines but not so to surface ships.

When I returned to Washington in the early nineties, after my tour in San Diego, I headed a staff developing the Navy budget. Much of our time was spent consolidating consensus positions among my fellow air, surface, and submarine flag officers. When the Cold War ended in 1991, the dollars supporting the defense budget dramatically fell, and the situation, while stressful, also provided an opportunity for thoughtful changes. Consequently, decommissioning all the nuclear surface ships was one of the measures the Secretary of the Navy used to balance his budget. I personally briefed the Office of Naval Reactors in advance on this decision. It was a rudder change for the Navy as it searched for open waters. Although making the surface force completely conventionally powered was counter to the position he had advocated, I thought Admiral Rickover would have been pleased that safety considerations and the challenge of old assumptions had driven the new conclusion.[7]

Another Change of Course: Restructuring the Submarine Force after the Cold War

The day Rickover died, a third of the ships in the Navy were submarines, not because he was such an exceptional lobbyist, but because of the facts. Undersea platforms were able to avoid Soviet submarine and air defenses and to carry the offensive directly against the Soviet mainland. Presidents understood and appreciated this, even if the military services did not. As is only belatedly recognized, Rickover's contribution to the U.S. victory in the Cold War was perhaps his greatest achievement.

However, in 1991, when the Soviets announced they were quitting, the Navy, which had been secretly monitoring the Soviets' internal communications, realized the Soviet Union was truly collapsing.[8] We therefore began a two-year review to restructure for future, non–Cold War threats. The first problem the submarine force faced was that we were building the wrong submarine. If the Soviets were out of business, then there was no need for the expensive submarine currently in production, the Seawolf class. This submarine had been designed to maneuver close to the Soviet coast, where no one else could go, and duplicate, with cruise missiles, the firepower of an aircraft-carrier strike.

In the world without a Soviet Union, carriers, no longer pitted against its hundreds of submarines, could operate much more freely. Consequently, to avoid overlapping missions, a less-expensive nuclear submarine was needed to operate in littoral (shallow, near-to-land) waters and conduct spy and intrusive missions. To design this new boat and keep a submarine production base warm,[9] the submarine component of the Navy proposed to terminate the new Seawolf class (SSN-21) and build a submarine designed for the post–Cold War world.[10] To free up funds for the research and development efforts necessary for this new submarine, the Navy proposed reducing the number of commissioned attack submarines by more than half.[11]

As you might suspect, the afternoon Vice Adm. Dan Cooper and I briefed Admiral Rickover's old organization on Cooper's plan to cut the number of attack submarines in half and also terminate the Seawolf class at three (instead of the larger number previously authorized by Congress), some in Naval Reactors were strongly convinced Cooper had lost his mind.

But Vice Admiral Cooper's plan was also the plan of Vice Adm. Bill Owens, the submariner responsible for the overall Navy's plans and policy, and of Frank Kelso, who was then the Chief of Naval Operations.[12]

Twenty-five years later the Virginia-class submarine, at a cost much more affordable than the Seawolf, is a great success, and its construction is maintaining the desired industrial base. It represented another complete course change, vehemently opposed by Naval Reactors in the moment yet completely consistent with the culture Rickover had installed of doing what was right. Rickover taught culture well.

Decommissioning the nuclear surface ships and launching the Virginia-class submarine happened more than two decades ago. Subsequently, I was busy with my non-Navy career—until one day it came to my attention that Admiral Rickover's culture was still particularly vibrant and strong in the submarine force.

Cultural Changes: Women in Submarines

In the fall of 2010, a brief note that the first class of twenty women would soon be entering nuclear training for assignments to submarines appeared in the *Washington Post*. Although several decades earlier I, and nearly every other senior submariner, had pressed hard for this change, we had lost the political battle. It was no longer my problem or my issue. I turned the page to read an article about the new pitcher for the Washington Nationals baseball team.

But as chance would have it, one of the outstanding women being admitted was the cousin of Audrey Noonan, who worked with me, and one afternoon, during my daily walk around the company, Audrey stopped me with a question: "Mr. Oliver, were you ever in submarines?"

"Yes . . ." I got no further, for her pent-up irritation literally burst forth—

"My cousin is an outstanding woman! Why should she go into submarines where they obviously don't want her?" Audrey's voice is normally quiet, but her tone was rising as was the blush in her cheeks. "Why should my cousin throw her talents away?" I could tell her lips badly wanted to add the words "on you pigs" at the end of her last phrase. She apparently only held back as a sop to my delicate sensitivities.

I spent a few moments trying to explain that the submarine culture was perfect for women. I emphasized that Admiral Rickover valued performance above everything else and had made a woman supervisor a critical part of his team in the early 1950s.[13] But I made little progress. Audrey did not recognize the name "Rickover." So, I invited Audrey and her cousin to lunch at our house. A few weeks later Audrey and her boyfriend came to lunch, along with her cousin, Jennie, and Jennie's father, who was driving the new trainee down to Charleston, South Carolina, to commence her career there at the nuclear training center.

I tried to use the lunch to explain to Jennie what an extraordinary career she might be lucky enough to experience. I wanted to make clear that the great majority of senior submariners had politically pushed for thirty years to get women into submarines. Nearly all submarine flag officers realized we needed brains to make the submarine force successful, and that women possessed half of the available resource. The delay in accessing women into submarines had not been the result of difficulties of gender or inadequate facilities on board the submarines but rather the resistance of a few submarine reprobates and their political allies. Jennie was proof that the culture Rickover had established had over time solved the political factors. It had taken much too long, but . . .

My wife and I served a good lunch, and there is always the distraction of memorabilia lying around the house of a couple who spent thirty years in the military. Jennie and her father wanted to be polite to Audrey's boss but were also eager to get on their way to Charleston and the beginning of Jennie's new life. I think my spouse and I successfully portrayed that submarines welcomed women, but the limited time constrained our conversation.

As our guests drove away, I was disappointed that I had not managed to convey to Jennie how special the culture of nuclear submarines is and how unique the man who had built the realm she was poised to enter.[14] I simply had not been adequately prepared. The two people, both deceased, by whom I still evaluate myself are my father and Admiral Rickover. Neither would have been impressed with my luncheon performance. My father never cursed me. I could not say the same for the good admiral.

But Rickover instilled a successful culture of management that has outlasted his name.

Afterword: Memorial Day

*We should value the faculty of knowing what we ought to do
and having the will to do it. Knowing is easy; it is the doing
that is difficult. The critical issue is not what we know
but what we* do *with what we know. The great end of life
is not knowledge, but action.*[1]

I am completing this on Memorial Day, a few miles from Admiral Rickover's gravesite in Arlington Cemetery, which looks over Washington, D.C. I think it only natural to reflect for a few pages on the context of his achievements.

In reviewing his professional accomplishments, we should consider two overlapping milieus. One is the threat to U.S. survival during his lifetime. The second is the spectacular effect his efforts had on our contemporary history. The American conflicts that occurred immediately following World War II, from 1946 to 1991—including the Korean War, the Berlin airlift, the Bay of Pigs, the Cuban Missile Crisis, the Vietnam War, the Nicaraguan secret war, and the Grenada invasion—while deadly serious for the millions of men and women involved, did not threaten the survival of the United States. They were rather rocky shoals piercing the ocean's surface in what seemed at the time to be an unending philosophical, economic, political, and military Cold War struggle between communism and capitalism.

In the larger Cold War battle, the communist bloc (that is, the Soviet Union and China) possessed a strong-to-overwhelming advantage in every aspect of the military dimension except for the Americans' ever-tenuous lead in nuclear weapons. The Soviets had much, much larger European armies as well as more armor and airplanes. In addition, they had a significant strategic advantage. Their armies were massed right on the borders of many of the Allies, whereas the Soviet Union's buffer of satellite countries prevented an instant counterstrike into the heart of the Soviet Union.

Thus, while it was impossible for the United States to mount any blitz attack on the Soviet homeland, the West remained vulnerable to Soviet attack. Our ground forces in West Germany knew they would be overwhelmed in hours or days if the Red Army ever chose to advance. The same situation existed on the other side of the world, in Seoul, South Korea. The only protection for these American and allied forces was nuclear retaliation, or as it was known at the time, mutual assured destruction, along with the necessary will to use this capability.

The one bright spot in the allied military equation was that the United States and Great Britain had larger, more capable navies. But this advantage had limited utility. It is not easy for navies to influence land powers, especially large ones such as the Soviet Union and China. In addition, the hundreds of Soviet submarines were intended to counter any allied naval ability to project force into Europe or Asia. Soviet submarines were more than capable of denying our surface ships and aircraft carriers access to the coastal areas of the Soviet mainland—shores also protected by miles of thick-pack ice during much of the year. The Cold War was a tense period. The United States could not reach out and touch, as military people euphemistically like to say, the Soviet Union, except with nuclear weapons.

This situation began to change as Adm. Hyman G. Rickover oversaw the successful development of the nuclear submarine, and in the process he gathered a team of people that would inculcate a system of continuous improvement into submarines. The technical breakthrough he oversaw was so significant and the cultural change he imposed was so vast that a few years after the submarine *Nautilus*' first underway in 1954, nuclear power had transformed an auxiliary warship of World Wars I and II into a stealth platform that ruled the oceans and unbalanced the Cold War.

With nuclear submarines, the United States controlled the surface as well as what moved in the waters below the sea. Our submarines could lie submerged nearly anywhere for as long as they liked, no matter what forces were arrayed against them. The nuclear submarine could do the bidding of the president of the United States anywhere in the world there was water. A warship that had been an afterthought in previous history became, with nuclear power, the point of the spear of the Cold War—and despite desperate efforts, the Soviets never caught up.

Soon, shrouded in secrecy, *Nautilus*' successors could penetrate any and all underwater defenses the Soviets could develop. With the culture Rickover established, American submarines became so technically advanced that they were essentially invulnerable. Even when the Soviets used traitors and spies to steal our communication codes, they could not counter our nuclear-submarine fleet.

Rickover and the Navy built such a superior platform that U.S. nuclear submarines could go under the ice and into Soviet waters at will. In addition, our submarines could and did track and target the Soviet ballistic-missile fleet (the Soviets' equivalent of our Polaris nuclear missile fleet) so that the Soviets knew their assured second-strike capability was placed at risk. The pressure finally affected the Soviet psyche. In December 1989 off Malta, when President Bush met with President Gorbachev on board the Soviet flagship *Gorki*, Marshal Sergei F. Akhromeyev handed President Bush the Soviet military leader's own morning intelligence report pictorial, shown in map 1. His accompanying words were significant: "We have read every one of your submarine messages for ten years and have been unable to find or kill even one of them. We quit."[2]

The Cold War was over. Theory X had finally proved correct.[3] Three years after Hyman Rickover's body had been laid to rest, his nuclear submarines had done their part in ensuring a grand theory of defense was able to protect American and Western values.

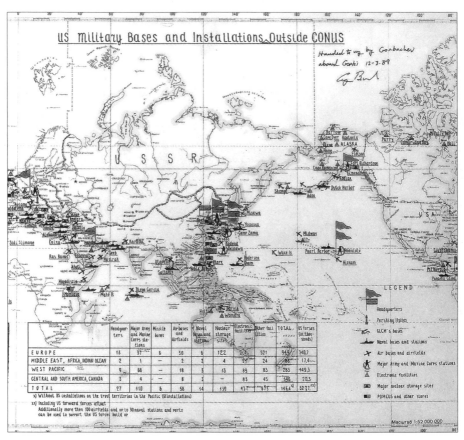

Map 1. Location of NATO military assets encircling the Soviet Union on 3 December 1989. The words in the upper-right corner read, "Handed to me by Gorbachev aboard Gorki. 12-3-89 (signed) George Bush." This copy hangs in my bedroom. I gave smaller copies to all the submarine commanding officers who worked for me at Submarine Group Five.

Notes

Chapter 1. Why Rickover Is Important

1. See Nilsen, Kudrik, and Nitkin, "Russian Northern Fleet Nuclear Submarine Accidents." Also see World Nuclear Association, "Nuclear-Powered Ships"; and Johnston, "Deadliest Radiation Accidents."

2. There are three particularly excellent biographies of Rickover: Duncan, *Rickover: The Struggle for Excellence*; Polmar and Allen, *Rickover*; and Rockwell, *Rickover Effect*. Two of these biographies were written by men who worked directly for the admiral. The third was written by a more critical duo. The admiral had a full life, and no one book can do it justice. My contribution focuses on the admiral's leadership and management style.

3. Ignoring the question of which nation originated which technology and focusing solely on the Americans involved passage through the air and under the water became contemporaneously feasible at the turn of the last century. The Wright brothers' first flight of their heavier-than-air machine was in 1903, and the U.S. Army bought its first aircraft five years later. Meanwhile, in 1900 John Holland beat out Simon Lake (my great-granduncle) in the Navy's competition to buy its first submarine.

4. Rickover, *Pepper, Rice, and Elephants*. This book was published three years after Ruth Rickover died. The author's foreword is dated December 1954, the year USS *Nautilus* was launched.

5. Rickover, "Thoughts on Man's Purpose."

Chapter 2. Challenges Rickover Faced

1. The "chipmunk" phrase is included in one of the admiral's statements to Diane Sawyer in his fifteen-minute *60 Minutes* interview in 1984. The session was filmed after Rickover had been forced to retire and was noteworthy for both him and Sawyer. It was her first television interview in what would become an exceptional professional career, and Rickover broke his long-standing aversion to *60 Minutes*, which he had previously maintained cut the tape to produce a result that supported the producers' personal bias.

2. According to Ted Rockwell (*Creating the New World*, 337), "Science is unparalleled in its ability to analyze a wide range of physical phenomena. But it is not the only way of thinking. . . . Admiral Rickover's approach to these things was intuitive and instinctive. In discussions over technical issues his arguments were seldom straightforward, rational or even valid. Often, after a bitter argument, events would take an unexpected turn, and Rickover's position would prove to be correct. 'Why do you guys fight me on stuff like this?' he would ask. We would try to explain that none of the facts seemed, at the time, to support his conclusion. 'But now you tell me I was right. Why am I always right for the wrong reasons?'"

3. There are many recent writings on this particular revolution in warfare, including Lecaque, "Guns That Almost Won." Also see Bilby, *Revolution in Arms*.

4. "Whether you like it or not, history is on our side. We will dig you in. We will bury you!" said Soviet premier Nikita Khrushchev in an address before Western ambassadors at a reception at the Polish embassy in Moscow on 18 November 1956. Cited in *Time*, "We Will Bury You."

5. Polmar and Allen, *Rickover*, 114.

6. As related to me by Medal of Honor winner (and the man who sunk the most Japanese tonnage during World War II) Vice Adm. Gene Fluckey during a visit he and his spouse made in 1984 to Yokosuka, Japan. The Japanese had invited the admiral to Japan to help them locate some of the ships he had sunk during the war. While researching, the Fluckeys stayed in the Submarine Sanctuary living area, which belonged to Submarine Group Seven.

7. John Cromwell, Sam Dealey, Gene Fluckey, Howard Gilmore, Dick O'Kane, Red Ramage, and George Street—these seven men were all awarded the Medal of Honor in the Pacific.

8. According to Valor at Sea, "U.S. Submarine Losses in World War II," "A total of 52 submarines were lost, with 374 officers and 3,131 enlisted men. . . .

    • The United States submarine service sustained the highest mortality rate of all branches of the U.S. Military during WWII

    • 1 out of every 5 U.S. Navy submariners was killed in WWII"

Chapter 3. Planning for Success

1. Rickover, speech delivered to Naval Postgraduate School.

2. It is extraordinary that Rickover was able to overcome his introversion as well as he did. To judge the extent of this characteristic, see Blair, *Atomic Submarine*, about Rickover's experiences as a submarine executive officer: "As time passed, however, conditions on the S-48 went from bad to worse for Rick. He and the commanding officer did not see eye to eye. Moreover, some of the men did not believe Rick was the sort of happy-go-lucky submarine officer they wanted to follow. He stubbornly refused to go ashore and associate with the other officers when the S-48 was on a cruise. He preferred to take lone exploration trips to the interiors of the foreign countries they visited, or spend his spare time studying more Naval War College correspondence courses" (p. 53). In a personal conversation in early 2012, Ted Rockwell, Rickover's first senior engineer, told me that Blair wrote his book from an office in Naval Reactors' spaces with editorial assistance from Ruth

Masters Rickover. Rockwell was spearheading an effort to get Rickover promoted from captain to admiral, and he planned to use Blair's book and articles
for that purpose. One would thus suspect the book presented the admiral in as
favorable a view as possible.

3. John Wayne was the submarine commanding officer in the very popular World
   War II movie *Operation Pacific* (1951).
4. It is almost impossible to exaggerate what was acceptable at the time. I well
   recall a particular commanding officer who routinely drank excessively and
   also invited different women to share his spousal bed. He was an effective warrior, and for many years his excesses were largely ignored. Finally, he reached
   the professional breaking point when he managed to steer his submerged
   submarine into both Pacific shores—the coral of Japan and the rock of San
   Diego—during the same voyage. He was relieved.
5. Wilkinson, "Abandoning the *Darter*," 185.
6. From my personal experience, I know that well into his nineties, Admiral
   Wilkinson was still making money in the cutthroat California poker parlors.
7. Wilkinson played championship tennis throughout his Navy career. See his
   Reminiscences.
8. Wilkinson, *Reminiscences*, 105–11. They were firing captured German V-1
   rockets, or Loons, a predecessor to the Regulus program, which in turn would
   lead to the Polaris, Poseidon, and Trident programs.
9. The most recent demonstration of this was the difficulty in coordinating
   Defense, State, and Treasury during the 2003–13 Iraq War.

Chapter 4. Inadvertent Consequences

1. Rickover, "Getting the Job Done Right." (This article was based on a speech
   the admiral gave at Columbia University.)
2. The satellite-based Global Positioning System, which has so much effect on
   our daily lives, was originally developed by Dr. Ivan Getting of Raytheon to
   provide exact positioning information for mobile transcontinental missiles.
3. At this time all ballistic-missile submarines on patrol used the same codes, or
   "keys," so snoopy submariners could read the encrypted mail addressed to sister ships. In this case we did so without hesitation.
4. My younger brother, Tim, was Wegner's deputy, and I had served as the engineer on board *Nautilus*. Both of these facts tended to build my credibility with
   the Naval Reactors office.
5. Anderson, *Ice Diaries*, 194. Commander Anderson tells this story somewhat differently (e.g., Anderson deliberately maneuvered around Rickover to
   arrange the trip, and the admiral believed the trip too demanding for *Nautilus*)
   but closely enough to confirm the existence of the envelopes: "Sunday, June 8,
   1958 [departure date for the pole]. I knew Rickover as well as anybody did.
   . . . But I also knew how he felt about risking *Nautilus* to explore under the
   Arctic ice. I did not relish a surprise visit, especially today. . . .

   "I had not discussed our proposed operation with him. I assumed, however,
   that the Pentagon, the White House, or both had made him aware of the details
   by then. The polar trip did not come up at all in our cordial conversation.

"Then just before he rose to leave he did a most unusual thing. Without comment, Rickover handed me a small scrap of paper he retrieved from his suit pocket. He had written on it the simple phrase: 'If necessary to reduce primary system leakage, it is satisfactory to the Bureau of Ships to reduce the pressure from 1,600 p.s.i. [pounds per square inch] to 1,400 p.s.i.' He signed it 'H. G. Rickover.'"

6. Ibid., 162. "Aurand later said, when he first learned about the proposal, Admiral Hyman Rickover was against it, and understandably so. Many submarine people thought it would risk *Nautilus*, which was unquestionably true." Presidential aide Capt. Evan Peter Aurand was an aviator who worked with Anderson (in successfully bypassing the Pentagon and Rickover) to convince Eisenhower to approve the under-the-pole mission. Aurand would subsequently retire as a vice admiral.

Chapter 5. Talent Repercussions

1. Rockwell, *Rickover Effect*.
2. Rickover was the author of three books on education: *Education and Freedom* (1959), *Swiss Schools and Ours: Why Theirs Are Better* (1962), and *American Education, a National Failure: The Problem of Our Schools and What We Can Learn from England* (1963). *Education and Freedom* and *American Education* were collections of his speeches on the subject.
3. Anderson, *Ice Diaries*. Anderson planned on taking *Nautilus* under the pole well before he became the skipper: "I was already doing a lot of thinking about exactly how I would make my mark as captain of *Nautilus*. The more I thought, the more my mind steered me northward" (p. 42). He kept his thoughts secret, knowing he was only one of several seeking to distinguish themselves from the other extraordinary men in the nuclear-power program: "Commander Calvert and a couple of the other prospective nuclear submarine skippers were also dreaming of the Arctic. . . . There was one other consideration. I suspected that Admiral Rickover would reject the thought of taking a nuclear ship under ice so early in the nuclear submarine era. As it turned out, that suspicion later proved to be correct" (pp. 44, 45). Anderson fails to note that his submarine, as essentially the first nuclear prototype, was not nearly as capable as the submarines commanded by the other nuclear skippers.
4. Ibid., 154–62.
5. Eisenhower chose to answer the Soviet threat asymmetrically—with a disruptive technology instead of a direct competition—because he believed that directly meeting the Soviet challenge in space (the approach President Kennedy later selected) would involve a very expensive arms race.
6. Anderson, *Ice Diaries*, 166–68. All of those top-secret messages were still on board *Nautilus* ten years after the trip under the pole, in a file locked outside the engineer officer's bunk. I used to read them during the hours between fires and other casualties.
7. Ibid., 158. Ned Beach's Magellan voyage in USS *Triton* would prove to be successful, but Eisenhower's campaign to use this achievement to shape world opinion was crushed when an American U-2 was shot down well inside the Soviet Union and pilot Gary Powers failed to use his curare poison

pin. At the next meeting of the presidents, the four-power Paris summit, Khrushchev trumped Eisenhower's latest submarine triumph with accusations of a secret and illegal American overflight. Some of this insight was highlighted by Ingrid Beach, Ned's spouse, during a discussion she and I had on 8 November 2013.

8. Eight days after the announcement, USS *Skate*, a newer submarine under the command of Jim Calvert, crossed under the North Pole, an event that received little attention outside the submarine force. On a technical note, the Navy would not begin to build submarines actually designed to go under the ice until nine years after both *Nautilus* and *Skate* had passed beneath the pole.

9. Anderson, *Ice Diaries*, 305.

10. Ibid. "There was another stop I wanted to make while I was in Washington. I intended to pay my respects to Admiral Hyman Rickover and brief him on the ship's condition and what he had planned for her while we were under the ice. I suppose it was in my mind somewhere that I might gain his blessing for the probe. . . . To my surprise and with no pleasantries whatsoever, Rickover jutted out his jaw and, his eyes blazing, said angrily, 'You're going to take that ship up there and get into trouble and you are going to wreck this program'" (p. 83).

Chapter 6. Escaping Responsibility

1. Adm. Hyman G. Rickover, as quoted by Duncan, *Rickover and the Nuclear Navy*, 294.

2. Ibid., 63. "Rickover . . . was responsible for the initial sea trials for the propulsion plant. His practice, broken only twice because of serious illness, was to direct the trials in person."

3. USS *Thresher* was lost on 10 April 1963. *Thresher* was the first class of nuclear submarines built by the Portsmouth Naval Shipyard under the laissez-faire concept then in vogue at the Bureau of Ships. All five previous classes of nuclear submarines, as well as the one-of-a-kind *Nautilus* and *Seawolf*, had been designed at Electric Boat in Groton (New London), Connecticut, a private shipyard operated much more in consonance with Rickover's technical guidance.

4. This rivalry had come to a boil in 1949 with the Revolt of the Admirals, and the underlying issues had not simmered away. The aides to the admirals who had been figuratively beheaded as a result of the incident were now admirals themselves. Not surprisingly, the former aides had neither forgotten nor forgiven.

   For those unfamiliar with the 1949 revolt, immediately after splitting off from the Army, the newly formed Air Force had convinced President Truman's new secretary of defense, Louis A. Johnson, that the Air Force could win all future wars with strategic (primarily nuclear) bombing; thus, the Navy and Marine Corps were no longer necessary. Perhaps tempted by the promise that this method of fighting would be less expensive and result in fewer American casualties, Secretary Johnson agreed with these views and publicly verbalized them—the fight was on. This warfighting and philosophical crevice was temporarily bridged with words by the House Armed Services Committee and then sidetracked by the Korean War (in which no nuclear weapons were used). The basic argument boiled beneath the surface of Washington defense discussions for decades whenever money became limited. It also tended to arise whenever

Air Force or Navy supporters were in a snit. There are even experts who maintain this fissure still exists. See Barlow, *Revolt of the Admirals*.

5. In January 1968 *Seawolf* ran aground during a training exercise. She was doing a high speed at the time and literally tore her stern planes and rudder from the ship. She was extraordinarily lucky to survive, as the subsequent court-martial inquiry uncovered. (I was the inquiry recorder.)

6. I use the word *theoretically* advisedly, as there was a limit to the depth at which unaided human escape was practical (the escape trunks as constructed were a vestige from diesel-submarine days, when most diesel operations, as well as the overwhelming preponderance of the accidents, took place in relatively shallow water). However, nuclear submarines spent their time in water so deep escape was impractical, and in fact our training had been harming more people than we could expect to save. In the eighties we finally discontinued escape training.

7. A fid is a tool that has been used for centuries on board ships to splice manila, and now nylon, lines (the naval term for the thick ropes used to lash the ship in place in port or next to another ship). The pointed end of the stretched, cone-shaped, smooth wood tool is forced (usually using a leather palm to protect the hand) between the strands of the line to open up the rope so that individual strands may be braided around the core of the line. Because it did not cut, a wooden fid was a useful tool when working with the rubber gaskets found in some valves as well as all watertight doors and hatches.

8. This event was reported in an early book about Admiral Rickover and Naval Reactors, and I suspect Admiral Rickover was the source. "On another trial a leak appeared to develop in a double-hatch leading to the deck. Rickover was convinced that the hatch was not leaking and that the water found between the hatches had resulted from an improper alignment of valves. When the commanding officer appeared reluctant to proceed, Rickover climbed into the space between the hatches with a flashlight while the ship submerged. Had there been a leak, there would have been no way to remove Rickover from the space between the hatches until the ship surfaced. Now more concerned than ever, the commanding officer took the ship down while Rickover made his point." Hewlett and Duncan, *Nuclear Navy: 1946–1962*, 338. Despite the book title I presume the event actually happened in 1966.

Chapter 7. The Danger of Culture

1. Adm. Hyman G. Rickover, speech delivered at Columbia University, 1982; govleaders.org/rickover.htm.

2. Romig, *Fatal Submarine Accidents*. The seven ships were E-2, O-5, K-4, S-49, SS-365 (*Cochino*), SS-464 (*Bass*), and SS-486 *(Pomondon)*.

3. The 1MC is a submarine communications system used to broadcast critical communications throughout the ship.

4. Admiral Rickover was not responsible for this inaction and inattention. He was limited by law to directing issues involving only the nuclear portion of the ship. As a consequence, in the fifties, sixties, and seventies, frustration with the lack of action from the nonnuclear portion of the Bureau of Ships was palpable at all levels in the submarine force. As a junior officer I could pick up the

telephone, call the appropriate office in Naval Reactors—or even the admiral himself, if I felt like living dangerously—and receive an answer to a technical question within a few hours. However, if I had an important problem in a portion of the ship that did not fall under the responsibility of the Kindly Old Gentleman, I would have to write a letter via the seven levels of command to the nonnuclear portion of the bureau and send it off into the ether—and months or years later, still nothing would have happened.

Finally, late one evening in the early seventies, while cursing and reading through the many volumes of the Bureau of Ships manual, I discovered an interesting paragraph. While I could not myself make any alteration to the ship without the Bureau of Ships approval, in an emergency I could make "an alteration in lieu of a repair" to the ship. All I had to do to make this legal was to promptly notify the bureau via the chain of command.

I remember rereading the paragraph several times. The wording did not define the level of emergency. I also remember leaning back in my chair and looking at the list of current engineering problems taped above my desk. A rational person would surely accept that on *Nautilus* I was dealing with an emergency each and every day. In fact, at that very moment I had nearly thirty unresolved requests to the bureau for nonnuclear alterations, and not one bureaucrat had yet seen fit to even say boo in reply. The one that irritated me the most was a four-hundred-cycle electrical generator located underneath a lithium bromide air-conditioning drain. With great care and a lot of work, we could get the electrical machine working for only a couple of days before something happened and the motor was once again drenched with seawater. The remainder of the time, the electrical unit was either on fire or bagged in plastic, waiting to be removed and repaired.

The next day I declared an emergency and moved the generator forty feet aft to a dry location above the main shaft. I filled out, signed, and mailed away all the necessary paper, positive the silent bureau would never respond. Soon we had accomplished most of the other changes for which we had previously requested approval.

I will not pretend that no displeasure was expressed during the next annual review of my records, performed by five members of the staff for the Atlantic commander in chief (the same fleet commander who I believed had been less than diligent in answering my mail). And I won't pretend we passed that inspection. However, ultimately, none of my people died—and the chain of command started paying attention to what I wanted to change.

5. For example, see Offley, *Scorpion Down*.
6. Kennedy, "Another Theory on Loss." "CNO SCORPION Technical Advisory Group . . . 28 Oct 2009. . . . The USS SCORPION was lost because hydrogen produced by the . . . main storage battery exploded in two-stages one half second apart. . . . This assessment is not the generic attribution of the loss of a submarine to a battery-explosion advanced as a default explanation in the absence of any more likely construct. . . . July 2008 reanalysis of the SCORPION 'precursor' acoustic signals. . . . The general battery damage is violent. The high velocity intrusion of pieces of the flash arrestor into both inside and outside surfaces of the retrieved plastisol cover attest to violence in

the battery well. . . . The battery probably exploded at some time before flooding of the battery well occurred."

Also see Polmar, "Re: 'Loss of USS *Scorpion*,'" 141, which is a comment on both the truth that a battery explosion caused the loss and the reluctance of some to accept facts.

7. For years the submarine force endured the problem of the standard operating practices diesel submariners brought with them to nuclear ships. The practices may have been well suited for diesel boats operating in shallow waters, yet frequently, they were completely inappropriate for the nuclear-submarine environment. Unfortunately, tradition so often trumps innovation that it took nearly two decades for us to weed out what was inappropriate. One of the corrective effects of Rickover's policy of drastically limiting the acceptance of diesel submariners directly into the nuclear ranks (and his accompanying preference for recruiting from the college ranks) was that fewer inappropriate diesel-boat processes needed to be uprooted.

8. Bentley, Thresher *Disaster*, 323.

9. As Adm. Frank Kelso, nuclear submariner and Chief of Naval Operations from 1990 to 1994, said about Admiral Rickover, "He was the most impersonal man I ever met. There isn't anyone even close to him. So that's hard to live with, but it probably meant he made pretty good decisions about people because he saw them all the same way. He didn't see them differently. You don't have favorites or non-favorites much." Kelso, *Reminiscences*, interview 4, 181.

Also read Schratz, "Admiral Rickover," for a contemporary view of how key individuals viewed Rickover's personality: "Rickover . . . was resented as a loner, a cutthroat with an abrasive personality. . . . Used the exploding technology of nuclear power to project his own career. . . . The cold, unrelenting, ruthless workaholic, undermining the bureaucracy . . . organized to the smallest detail, intolerant of error, devoting everything including his personal life to a cause." Dr. Schratz, who achieved command (of USS *Pickerel* [SS-524]) shortly after World War II, reviewed many books for the Naval Institute after he had retired from serving as a diesel submariner. Some suspect that because of his key position, Schratz had a biased but nevertheless critical role in determining how Rickover was viewed by the general readership of this respected and Navy-focused organization. Dr. Schratz died in 1993, seven years after Admiral Rickover passed.

Chapter 8. Future Shadows

1. Rickover, speech delivered to Naval Postgraduate School.

2. For example, he had not sought even the most minor leadership role during his years at the Naval Academy. According to Duncan (*Rickover: The Struggle for Excellence*, 16), "Although he had no desire to hold rank in the regiment, in the academic year 1920–21 Rickover was second petty officer, 4th Battalion, largely because the superintendent had decided that all midshipmen insofar as possible would receive some training in the handling of men." Also see Blair, *Atomic Submarine*, for several interesting comments about how, as a young officer, Rickover would rather do practically anything than participate in a social function.

3. S1W was the designation of the first submarine training prototype. The "S" was for submarine and the "W" for the contractor who built the trainer. The manufacturer for this prototype reactor and engineering plant (as well as for USS *Nautilus*) was Westinghouse. The next major trainer built in Idaho would be A1W, with the "A" in this case standing for aircraft carrier, as this unit would be the prototype for USS *Enterprise*. The *Enterprise* reactor was also built by Westinghouse.

4. Observing evolutions involved monitoring an individual doing a routine action to ensure it was being done completely correctly and the individual knew why each particular step in the process existed.

5. If Admiral Rickover had previously approved an officer for his particular duty (a group which on a submarine normally included the commanding officer, executive officer, and engineer officer), these officers were not subsequently "inspected" by this team. Rather, we "certified" officers observed the examination as our work in preparing the ship's crew was judged. The inspection was intended to evaluate whether the senior officers were adequately performing their primary role of training. Not evaluating those whom Rickover had already certified emphasized to everyone, including those on his staff, that Rickover was firmly in charge. No one got the impression that any mere staff member was capable to judge what the admiral had already approved. Of course, as will come to light when I discuss Operating Instruction 62 in chapter 11, this emphasis had its downsides.

Chapter 9. Knowing You, Knowing Me

1. Nixon, "Remarks at a Promotion Ceremony."

2. Song lyrics to "Martha," performed by Tom Waits. Copyright Elektra/Asylum Records, 1985.

3. At that time nuclear submarines had a little red phone directly connected to the White House switchboard. By simply picking up the receiver, you could be in personal conversation with the president of the United States. How cool!

4. W. Edwards Deming was a statistician who is often credited as the Father of Quality Control. He built the Japanese automobile business after World War II (by producing automobiles much more reliable than those produced in the United States) and then was hired to return home and teach his techniques in Detroit. This in turn resulted in a resurgence of the American automobile industry. Deming was a contemporary of Rickover's.

5. Wegner interviewed me for nine hours before Rickover would permit me to serve as engineer on board USS *Nautilus*. It actually was a one-on-two interview as Wegner was asking reactor-plant technical and operational questions of two young lieutenants. When we were all three exhausted, Wegner turned to me.

   "Do you want East or West Coast duty?"

   Demonstrating remarkably good judgment, I replied, "I need to call my wife."

   Mr. Wegner, who on some occasions showed the impatience Rickover was famous for, said, "There is no time for that. You are now the engineer on *Nautilus*. Report to New London [Connecticut]."

He completed our session by turning to Bill Owens (who some years later would become the vice chairman of the Joint Chiefs of Staff): "You go west. You are the new engineer on *Seadragon*." (USS *Seadragon* [SSN-584] was another of the early submarines experiencing engineering difficulties during this period.)

Before I left that day, Rickover had given me his home telephone number (by which I could, if I dared, bypass the nine levels of Navy command between the two of us). With the insight the *Nautilus'* challenges would provide me and my subsequent contact with Rickover, I grew to believe I understood him as well as anyone but Ruth and Eleonore.

6. Subsequently, the Marine Corps and Special Warfare have adopted a similar system using a more junior officer to conduct the interview.

Chapter 10. Wooing and Winning

1. Rockwell, *Rickover Effect*, 133.

2. For a period in the seventies, when it looked as if the Equal Rights Amendment to the Constitution might pass, Rickover interviewed and trained women. Only thirty-five of the necessary thirty-eight states had ratified the amendment by 1982, and the amendment ultimately expired. Subsequently, since Congress had specifically decreed that women could not serve on submarines, most of the female applicants served in nonsubmarine jobs involving controlling radioactivity exposure. A decade later, in 1994, Naval Reactors began assessing women for service in nuclear-powered surface ships, and in 2010 twenty women were recruited for nuclear-submarine training.

3. When I had my initial interview, it was relatively late one February afternoon, and the windows in Admiral Rickover's office were already dark. The brightest light in the room was an old desk lamp. The accordion metal gooseneck bent in nearly a *U* held a shielded single bulb so the older man (he was already sixty-three) could clearly see the top page of the pile of papers he was reading. His red pen was circling items he had questions about. When he came to a stopping point, I realized the meager brown file on his desk was probably my personal record. I surmised it included my academic transcript, probably also my trio of Class As (Naval Academy slang for court-martials), each documenting a slightly different form of insubordination (I would have valiantly tried to explain if he had only cared to ask), as well as the three interviews I had completed with different individuals on his staff earlier in the day.

The admiral spoke, "You are about to graduate as the first literature major in the history of the Naval Academy—so write down the titles of the last ten books you have read."

I quickly wrote down nine and handed him the list. They were a mixture of novels, plays, and contemporary international relations commentaries. I am certain the list contained only nine because I had been reading *Lady Chatterley's Lover* the previous evening and could not excise Constance from my mind. I do and did have some minimal judgment, and thus that particular book did not make the paper I handed the admiral.

My single sheet of paper rested under the gooseneck lamp between his two small hands. He read without picking it up and then leaned back slightly from the only light in the rapidly darkening room. His high-pitched voice began, and for the next half hour, this admiral, this man who was the Father of Nuclear Power, responsible for managing a brand new engineering science, leisurely summarized the concepts each of my authors had avowed. In two cases Rickover chose to emphasize a point he believed the authors should have more clearly identified, and in one book that had captured his fancy, he paraphrased the author's opening paragraph as well as a key passage.

By the time he reached the ninth line, the heat from the single lightbulb had begun to curl up the top and bottom of my list, and Rickover had snared another set of hands to help build a future only the admiral envisioned. So far, my interview had not yet required me to say a single word, much less recall an engineering principle. In fact, the admiral was still speaking: "I read a great deal. My wife summarizes those books when I do not have time. You will find that anyone can study literature and history by themselves, but," and he looked down as his right hand closed on and crumpled my list, "you need a professor to help you when you are studying mathematics and engineering, or you will make mistakes."

He looked up at me. "Do you understand?"

"Yes, Sir."

"Get out of here."

I followed my host (an officer about to go to a nuclear-submarine command who was forbidden to help you decide to grow up) to an outside office. Once there, I asked him what he recommended I do. He replied with a refrain I would later learn was one of the admiral's favorites: "Do what you think is right."

A couple of hours later, at a break in initial interviews, I returned to see the admiral and told him that for the last semester at the Naval Academy, I was going to substitute nuclear physics and the sixth year of college mathematics for the six credit hours I had previously set aside for literature and history. The admiral nodded but said nothing more. After the bus had returned to Annapolis that evening, I found I was on the list of students the admiral had accepted for nuclear power.

4. "He wanted straight, honest, and brief answers. . . . He did not want any 'yes men' around. He was tough on accepting personnel for training. . . . He was interested only in those men he believed would seriously concentrate on learning and could be relied upon to produce desired results." Summitt, *Tales of a Cold War Submariner*, 198.

5. Rockwell, *Rickover Effect*, 237.

6. "I was spending the majority of each day at BuPers [the Bureau of Personnel] screening service records to identify candidates for Rickover to consider for nuclear-power training. I sought officers with excellent fitness reports who had performed well in college. Rickover did not seem to care what a person had studied in college as long as he had been a good, dedicated and serious student.

" . . . Selecting candidates based solely on the strength of their records was not enough. He wanted to interview each and every one to see what they were made of and if he thought they had what it took to successfully qualify. He saw no sense in wasting time and money on anyone he did not judge capable of being successful." Summitt, *Tales of a Cold War Submariner*, 197, 198.

7. From Duncan, *Reminiscences*, 839: "The officer involved had been nuclear-qualified, he'd been a nuclear submarine engineer, he'd been executive officer in a nuclear submarine, and he had glowing fitness reports. I think on his record I'd have said 'go,' Admiral Rickover called him in for an interview and turned him down. So the submarine desk [it comprised diesel submariners] thought they had a case. Some officers said rather extravagant things like, 'we'll take this one to Congress,' which frankly was a silly thing to think of thinking. But in any event I just use this because I was there. Admiral Smedberg [chief of naval personnel from 1960 to 1964 who did not hide his dislike of Rickover] and I decided maybe we'd better talk to this officer and so we sent for him. He hadn't been in the room five minutes before Admiral Smedberg and I realized the fellow was practically in the middle of a nervous breakdown and couldn't possibly be given command of a submarine. But the Bureau officers had not had access to him.

"Q: They had paper access?

"Admiral Duncan: They had paper access."

Chapter 11. Innovation and Process

1. Rockwell, *Rickover Effect*, 85.
2. Dave Minton's historical 1972 patrol on board USS *Guardfish* (SSN-612) was one of the notable exceptions.
3. The pressure to participate in Vietnam was strong. In 1966, in response to a Navy-wide appeal, I volunteered for command of a riverboat in the Mekong Delta, only to soon receive a letter from Admiral Rickover saying my services were required in the submarine force. At the time I had no need to know what our attack submarines were doing against the Soviet Union (at the time I was attached to a ballistic-missile submarine), so I naturally railed at the decision.
4. Just as continual improvement is the hallmark of any successful business. What Rickover was teaching would eventually be recognized as essentially the same *Kaizen* process Deming concurrently was introducing in Japan.
5. Make no mistake: the conflict between diesel and nuclear submariners was somewhat akin to a religious war, for nonnuclear submariners viewed nuclear submariners the way missionaries do the poor souls who fail to "see the light" and nuclear submariners of course felt the same about their nonnuclear counterparts. Just as in a religious war, there was not much room for compromise— or even unimpassioned discussion.
6. I had a pleasant back-and-forth tête-à-tête with Deming after one of his lectures in Chicago. He told me that organizations will always include a certain number of people who are out of control—that is, their performance is so unique as not to be explainable by any statistical analysis—and that these few individuals are essential to innovation—but necessarily need to be few.
7. The Maginot line was the famous series of fortifications France erected at the direction of the French minister of war. The line was considered impenetrable (when approached from Germany) to the tanks and artillery of the time. In response, the Germans outfitted their tanks with radios, enabling a coordination not heretofore seen in battle and permitting the Germans to use their new maneuverability to leave their center exposed. This released forces to outflank

the Maginot line through the neutral countries Belgium, Luxembourg, and the Netherlands. The Germans then returned to the Maginot line from the French side after occupying Paris. The fortifications became another historical monument to the limitations of a static defense, the dangers of preparing for the last war, and the importance of militaries' attending to technology innovations.

8. I suspected I knew how this change came to be. About five years earlier, a turn-to-turn failure of a large electrical component had occurred on board *Nautilus*. The accompanying severe electrical surge had shut down, or *scrammed* in Navy parlance, the reactor. In the blink of an eye, the only light on board was from the electrical fire. Technically, the shutdown should not have happened. The electrical system breakers, which Rickover had designed during his World War II stint at the Bureau of Ships, were supposed to selectively trip (meaning the breaker closest to the problem should open first and leave the rest of the electrical system unaffected).

   Since I was supervising the engineering plant at the time and could picture in my mind all the meter readings in maneuvering as the lights went out, I knew the scram was not an operator error but instead an engineering flaw. After some effort, including a particularly dramatic test to replicate the problem, we found that during the previous overhaul Portsmouth Naval Shipyard had reversed the installation of key components in the breakers (our poor repairs had occurred five years after the shipyard had done a similar slipshod job on *Thresher*, so the new quality standards had not yet been fully assimilated there). As rebuilt, the breakers would not open properly when a problem occurred. In fact, the breakers wouldn't open until they literally melted. The new O/I 62 would ensure a similar problem never remained undetected.

9. The Goat Locker is the living space for the senior enlisted personnel (E-7 to E-9) on board a submarine.

10. I always appreciated this symbolic action, particularly since it turned out we had inadvertently included two typos in the couple of dozen procedural pages, and he issued it with those two typos intact. He didn't say, "This is from Dave, who cares about our sailors more than many of the rest of you," but by issuing the change with the typos, the chief and I felt we were receiving his personal approbation.

11. *Fitness report* is the term for the (usually annual) assessment of naval-officer performance. There are always consequences—for both actions and inactions. Much of life is deciding which consequences you wish to share your bed with at night when you lie down to sleep.

Chapter 12. Elephant Instincts

1. Rickover, "Doing a Job."

2. In addition to the ongoing Vietnam and Cold Wars (as well as the not-so quiet conflict between the U.S. Navy and the U.S. Air Force for air and nuclear supremacy within the U.S. military), the submarine portion of the Navy was also frothing with excitement. In March 1971 Admiral Zumwalt had appointed Vice Adm. Phil Beshany as the initial deputy chief of naval operations for submarines (for the first time placing submarines on a bureaucratic par with airplanes and surface ships in the Navy).

3. Soon afterward, because nuclear submarines were so often at sea for long periods and thus nuclear submarine officers did not have the opportunity to practice underways and landings nearly as much as their conventional counterparts, underways and landings began being routinely done with the assistance of tugs.

4. Mouza Coutelais-du-Roche Zumwalt, with whom my wife, Linda, became good friends.

5. McKee was executive officer of *Nautilus* in 1961, and it was definitely his handwriting in the Machinery History, but his signature on the page did not make sense. The work should have been overseen by the engineer or machinery division officer, not the executive officer. When I worked for him, our discussion of this subject was always interrupted by real-world events, so the details remain a mystery to me to this day. I only know the valves worked nicely when they were put back on the proper sides of the boat.

6. And the gentleman who did get this wonderful job as the first fellow subsequently was not selected for admiral. C'est la vie.

7. Like Rickover, Zumwalt had his own cover of *Time*, on December 21, 1970.

8. Many of the churches in Northern Virginia were segregated in the early seventies, and Mouza Zumwalt and my spouse would attend services together on Wednesday afternoons. They would sit with the black congregations in the back or in the lofts. Linda would come home each week crying about the injustice—this was my clue that Mouza had also gone home in tears and that the next day would see the Chief of Naval Operations redouble his efforts to eliminate segregation in the Navy.

9. See Zumwalt, *On Watch*, 85–95, for his recounting of his interview with Admiral Rickover for the nuclear-power program. For a completely different view of this same interview (and of Admiral Zumwalt), see Peet, *Reminiscences*, 163–68 (Zumwalt and Peet were interviewed together). Adm. Hal Shear (who was the Naval Reactors monitor for this particular interview) has comments on the event in his *Reminiscences* (159–60). I wasn't there for the interview but was present for two years while Zumwalt was Chief of Naval Operations. Zumwalt detested and was determined to best Rickover.

10. I always felt that wearing civilian clothes was a wise policy for Rickover during his captain and early admiral days, for this prevented people from focusing on how junior Rickover was in the Navy hierarchy (and everyone in Washington reads and understands the relative rank of officers). In addition, not wearing a uniform meant Rickover did not have to compete with other officers with respect to how many rows of combat ribbons he was wearing (another archaic realm of knowledge well understood within the Washington beltway).

Of course, this leaves open to question the issue of how well Rickover adapted to changing circumstances. Once he had been promoted in early 1973 to four stars and had received his first Congressional Gold Medal and Distinguished Service Medal, he was officially one of the eight or nine senior naval officers in the world, and no other active officer had a Gold Medal. I have always thought that wearing a uniform after his promotion most likely would have subconsciously helped bolster his arguments. Yet Rickover did not change his pattern—he remained in mufti as he had since he was a captain in the Navy—and thus gave away a position of power in the constant conflict with his detractors.

11. Friedman, *U.S. Submarines.*

12. The Trident was a product of a 1968 study about the next U.S. missile system (essentially a competition between the Air Force's recommendation for a Minuteman replacement and the Navy's proposal for a Polaris follow-on).

13. The DD-963 class destroyer would be a great success, and the FFG-7 frigate less so. Both were needed to fill the surface-ship gap resulting from the large numbers of World War II ships retiring after extended service in Vietnam. The surface-ship gap produced fiscal tension in the Navy between the money devoted toward submarine- and surface-force construction, tension that was exacerbated by an underlying inequity in the ascent of different warfare specialties to the chief of naval operations billet. Zumwalt was the first Chief of Naval Operations in some time who was a surface officer (the aviators made up more than 50 percent of the officers and thus most often served as chiefs of naval operations during this period). So while Rickover had convinced the president and Congress to fund submarines and the previous chiefs of naval operations had funded aircraft, surface ships had generally been neglected.

14. I learned a great deal about ship design (the Naval Ships Sea Command personnel understood this subject much better than I) but ended up simply removing one of the two (exceptionally expensive) graving docks and some other facilitation from the Bangor, Washington, construction plan.

15. Zumwalt is the last Chief of Naval Operations to have lived in the Naval Observatory on Massachusetts Avenue, NW, in Washington, D.C. When Admiral Zumwalt moved out, the house became the vice president's residence.

16. Subsequently, all the nuclear shipyards experienced expensive problems learning how to weld the new HY-130 steel without cracking—the precise process the construction of the NR-2 was intended to debug. Whether the welding processes would have matured sufficiently while building the $300 million NR-2 to avoid these later costs was the issue under discussion at the time.

17. A great number of Admiral Zumwalt's changes were successfully resisted, and many of those he established were countermanded within a few months of his retirement. This is not to say his cultural-change methods were inferior, for he had only four years in his leadership role and had a much larger group to influence, whereas Rickover had a small group and almost thirty years. Zumwalt, to his great credit, did irrevocably start the Navy down the path to face a new cultural future. From my personal observations of Admiral Zumwalt and Admiral Rickover, as well as an effort I participated in in the large public company Airbus (named EADS at the time), my conclusion is that achieving real cultural change takes something more than two years and less than ten. I feel confident in the bounds but not in any number more precisely refined.

18. In the early eighties two privately owned shipyards, Electric Boat and Newport News, had recently been bought by conglomerates (General Dynamics and Tenneco, respectively) and submitted claims to the Navy for large sums of money for cost overruns. Rickover did not feel these costs were justified and was active, publicly and emotionally, in recommending the requested sums not be paid. The story is complex, but it included fortunes for lobbyists, corporate secret meetings, congressional hearings, bribery, misconduct charges, and the fleeing of the Electric Boat CEO to Greece to avoid extradition. For

the most comprehensive report, see Tyler, *Running Critical*. Also see Duncan, *Rickover: The Struggle for Excellence*, 240–56. For a less extensive discussion, see Polmar and Allen, *Rickover*, 488–513.

Because Rickover was fighting tooth and nail not to pay the companies money they needed to maintain their stock prices, both companies desperately wanted Rickover out of office. The Reagan administration, represented by Secretary John Lehman, was committed to building the Navy up to six hundred ships. Secretary Lehman believed he needed the support of these two shipyards. However, ushering Rickover out was neither easy nor fun.

After Rickover had been forced into retirement, Electric Boat made up a list of the favors they had provided Rickover over the past twenty years (rides to and from the airport, etc.; a list valued at more than $67,000). The list included innocuous items such as box lunches, as well as other items the admiral had probably used as gifts to legislators. The list might not have been too damaging, but unfortunately, it also contained diamond earrings for his second wife (see Flynn, "Navy Penalizes GD"). Rickover was censured by the Secretary of the Navy (the same day the chairman of General Dynamics, owner of Electric Boat, resigned). The admiral's protests that "he had always acted in the best interest of the Navy and my country," while undoubtedly true, seemed to ignore the level of propriety that he had demanded of others. Some wondered if the comments by the eighty-five-year-old man were a part of the failure of his short-term memory noted by Duncan (*Rickover: The Struggle for Excellence*, 293). Also see Riddell, *Through My Periscope*, 281–84.

Chapter 13. Genetics

1. Rickover, "Thoughts on Man's Purpose."

2. Because nuclear submarines were so important in the Cold War and the Soviet fleet was more numerous than the American, there was a constant need for submarines to be at sea. An attack submarine has only one crew, so whenever the ship is at sea, so is its crew. During the Cold War most nuclear-attack submarines were away from their home port (and their families) for nearly 80 percent of each year. As you may suspect, these extended absences were not a positive retention tool, which meant even more sea duty for those of us who remained in submarines.

   This was the case for the entire Cold War. Consequently, some officers had been assigned to submarines for twenty years, with only two or three years not in an at-sea assignment (their surface and aviator peers had much less time away from their families). The amount of time submariners spent away from home was a matter of geography—the distance of each U.S. coast from the Soviet Union. In the Pacific, submarines deployed for over a year at a time (in the Atlantic, since the transit time was shorter, deployments were only six months). In general, attack-submarine life was not optimal for those men who had or wanted a family.

3. Frequently, in addition to the three months, one or more of the commanding officer candidates would require a week or two of special instruction before Rickover was satisfied.

4. After the nuclear accident at Three Mile Island, Pate, who in addition to being a truly exceptional naval officer also had a PhD in nuclear physics from the Massachusetts Institute of Technology, went to work at the Institute of Nuclear Power Operations as part of the team working to restore public confidence in commercial nuclear power in the United States. He eventually succeeded Adm. Dennis Wilkinson as the organization's president and CEO.

Chapter 14. Never Beat a Compass So True

1. Rickover, speech delivered to Naval Postgraduate School.
2. The lyrics are from the 1955 hit musical *Damn Yankees* (music and lyrics by Richard Adler and Jerry Ross), which took Broadway by storm the same year *Nautilus* was having an identical effect upon the world's navies.
3. See Beshany, *Reminiscences*, interview 7, for written confirmation of my recollection.
4. Although this was a subject of loud discussion at the time, it should have been evident that the precautions necessary in work involving possibly radioactive reactor systems were introducing new costs. In addition, Rickover had taught his acolytes to insist on performing a job properly or doing it again. This had not previously been the standard in nonnuclear ship repairs.
5. In the process the Navy then used for budgeting money, the people responsible for carrier maintenance had only to earmark money for the costs they estimated. If they therefore "honestly" estimated that the *Enterprise* overhaul would cost no more than a conventional carrier overhaul, then they had to put aside only that lower estimate in planning dollars (rather than a more reasonable expected sum of double or triple that number). Following this approach would magically provide planning money sufficient to overhaul another one or two carriers or, since money is fungible, to plan to buy more airplanes. The lowest possible ship overhaul estimate made these estimators popular people, and everyone enjoys being liked.
6. Since at that time submarine crews remained with their ships during overhauls, whereas the majority of the surface-ship crews did not, Bremerton was largely a submarine town. The housing situation was so dire that two young married couples lived with Linda and me and our two sons for over a year before the couples could find and close on their own homes.
7. Among those not interested in informing Rickover of possible trouble were his own people whom the admiral had inserted in each shipyard. Rickover's shipyard representatives were supposed to be alert to precisely this sort of problem and responsible for reporting it to him. This should amply demonstrate that all management systems depending on people will occasionally (or more often) either run amuck or, more likely, fail to recognize the precise situation they were installed to detect. Rickover taught that if one does not have at least three independent check systems for what is considered important, one does not have a system. However, often no number of independent checks will suffice to discover a problem people have previously never seen.
8. Overhaul tasks are controlled by a system subsequently known as the PERT (program evaluation and review technique) chart.

9. Reporting labor was also the method for charging work. Thus, if workers were erroneously reported to be working on ship A when they were actually working on ship B, then funds allocated by Congress (which provides a specific amount of money for each ship) were being subverted. In this case, funds were essentially being taken away from the submarine force and given under the table to the surface force or to aviation (an even more terrible offense in some Navy circles).

Chapter 15. Renaissance Man

1. Rickover, speech delivered to Naval Postgraduate School.
2. At the age of eighty-two, after having recovered from two heart attacks, Admiral Rickover found himself fighting the administration, industry, and the Navy regarding how to resolve his accusations of improper financial conduct by the Electric Boat shipyard (owned by General Dynamics) and the Newport News shipyard (then owned by Tenneco). The record indicates Rickover was correct, but nevertheless, he lost the argument (Tyler, *Running Critical*). Rickover was retired and died four years later. The companies were subsequently paid hundreds of millions of dollars most believe they did not deserve.
3. America's land-based missile fields and bomber forces were both susceptible to surprise attack, as the still blue waters of Pearl Harbor and simply the date of 7 December 1941 remind us.
4. In the forty years of the Cold War, except by accident, which the principle of "small ship, big sea" minimized, the Soviets never located an American fleet ballistic-missile submarine.
5. *At risk* was the euphemism used to describe the ability to destroy the Soviet ballistic-missile submarine at least before it had launched its second missile, and possibly before the first one left its tube.
6. We would later discover that the Soviets had established a set of American traitors within the Navy (the Walker-Whitworth ring). The information the traitors disclosed led the Soviets to alter their concept of submarine operations. These changes made our detection and tracking much more difficult.
7. The healthy submarine-building rate was not the result of Pentagon requests but rather of an unusual alliance between the White House and key members of Congress who were carefully briefed on submarine exploits.
8. During this at-sea period several difficult decisions had to be made. Several times my engineer officer recommended that we turn back or head for the nearest port. If I had not been nuclear trained, I might not have had the self-confidence in this demanding situation to say, "No, I fully understand the risks involved and have balanced them against the operational gains that may be made, and I take full responsibility. This is what we will do to compensate for this additional risk." I make the point because some other countries with nuclear submarines don't require their commanding officers to be nuclear trained. As a result, critics of the U.S. system use these other countries as examples to recommend the United States change its practices. The critics propose permitting people with less technical training and knowledge to serve as nuclear-submarine commanding officers. I am positive my ship would have

turned back empty-handed and failed in its mission if a nonnuc had been in command of *Plunger*.

9. Capt. Hank Chiles and his wife, Katy, were close friends. He was commanding officer of USS *Gurnard* in the other San Diego squadron. He had also made an exceptional Western Pacific deployment and been invited back to brief various commands in Washington. Chiles would later advance through the admiral ranks to the highest level and the role of commander in chief of the U.S. Strategic Command.

10. In 1972 Minton led one of the most extraordinary missions ever conducted (commonly referred to as the "Saga of the 1972 *Guardfish* Patrol"). He alerted the president to an impending nuclear attack and then simultaneously trailed three Soviet submarines from Vladivostok through thousands of miles of dangerous waters to Vietnam. Minton single-handedly prevented these Soviet submarines from targeting our carriers with their nuclear-tipped cruise missiles. He was every submariner's operational hero.

11. If you want another famous reference that participation or nonparticipation in sports was just something to talk about, read Wilkinson, *Reminiscences*. Wilkinson played tournament tennis throughout his Navy career; won many championships, including those of other services; and was a visible and proud athlete.

Chapter 16. Innovation and Change

1. Rickover, speech delivered to Naval Postgraduate School.

2. I believe this is both because the commentaries have been written by his critics (who saw no or negative value in Rickover's methods) and because the remaining histories have been written by men who worked closely with the admiral. The latter viewed nearly everything Rickover did as one does the actions of family members, whom one loves even when they are at their worst. I know of no histories of Rickover written by the men actually responsible for the operation of his submarines at sea, where Rickover's innovations changed the course of history. The men who were his critics, knowingly or not, were essentially siding with the opponents of the cultural changes Rickover viewed as critical to the technology shift from diesel to nuclear. The men on Rickover's staff were engineers. They accurately reported his tactical moves but were not emotionally or physically involved in the cultural changeover. As a consequence, this book deliberately ignores many of the aspects of Rickover's fascinating life in order to focus on what he contributed to the disciplines of management and leadership.

3. The surface nuclear fleet was decommissioned shortly after Rickover's death, for while nuclear power provides advantages to aircraft carriers that the Navy has decided are worth the added investment, nuclear power does not transform any surface ship's usefulness.

4. See Blair, *Atomic Submarine*, 46, for the following quote about Lieutenant (junior grade) Rickover's time on board the battleship *Nevada* in 1925: "Captain Kempff called him on the ship's telephone and urged that he attend a party staged by an admiral on a nearby flagship. . . . There was a great deal of crowding of the boats at the flagship's gangway as Navy brass from the many ships in the harbor gathered to go up the glistening ladder, through the

receiving line on the sparking quarterdeck and thence into the party below decks. At length Rickover's boat worked its way alongside the ship, and as he climbed on the boat, he whispered into the coxswain's ear. Seconds later, he scurried up the starboard ladder, zipped through the receiving line, firmly shook the Admiral's hand, kept walking straight to the other side of the ship, clambered down the port ladder and stepped into the waiting motor launch . . . within half an hour, he was back aboard the Nevada at work in the electrical office."

5. Especially telling to me is the fact that neither H. G. nor Ruth Masters Rickover realized that this passage from Blair (*Atomic Submarine*, 53) could be read as particularly damning for a man who wanted to be portrayed as a leader of men: "As time passed, however, conditions on the S-48 went from bad to worse for Rick. . . . Some of the men did not believe Rick was the sort of happy-go-lucky submarine officer they wanted to follow. He stubbornly refused to go ashore and associate with the other officers when the S-48 was on a cruise. He preferred to take lone exploration trips to the interiors of the foreign countries they visited, or spend his spare time studying more Naval War College correspondence courses."

6. Of course, Rickover was an extraordinary leader by John Kotter's definition (from his "What Leaders Really Do"): "Both [leaders and managers] are necessary for success in today's business environment. Management is about coping with complexity. Its practices and procedures are, for the most part, responses to the emergence of large, complex organizations in the 20th century. Leadership, by contrast, is about coping with change." But Kotter's view was not the accepted view of leadership by Rickover's admiral peers. It was not that there was or is a common accepted definition. The Navy saw no real need to establish one. The organization shared Supreme Court Justice Potter Stewart's pragmatism. They knew leadership when they saw it.

7. "[Rickover] reported aboard [*Finch*] early on the morning of July 17 [1937]. . . . Later that day Rickover relieved Lieutenant Joseph P. Rockwell, who, having served as commanding officer for less than a month, was hastily departing to become aide to the U.S. High Commissioner of the Philippines. . . . Rockwell had been put in command of the *Finch* at the specific direction of Admiral Yarnell, who . . . wanted to observe Rockwell close at hand before sending him on to the Philippines with his highest recommendations. . . . Rockwell considered her [*Finch*] the best of the five ships he commanded during his naval career.

"Evans relieved Rickover on October 5 [1937]. At the time the *Finch* was moored alongside the gunboat *Isabel*, at Shanghai. Evans, in turn, would command the *Finch* for only four months before he was relieved, carrying on the *Finch*'s tradition of changing commanding officers virtually with the seasons.

"Memories have been dimmed by more than four decades of time . . . but some officers on the Asiatic scene at the time vividly recall the *Finch*. Once, according to one officer, she was seen 'steaming into port with a red flag flying from her mast and the crew had painted "madhouse" on her side, in red.' . . . The words on her side were probably in 'red lead: as the crew repainted the ship and made sport of their conditions under Rickover.'" Polmar and Allen, *Rickover*, 84–90.

8. He was in the Pacific for a few months, assigned as the commander of the ship repair facility on Okinawa in July 1945, but one month later the atomic bombs were dropped on Hiroshima and Nagasaki, and the great war was over. Polmar and Allen, *Rickover*, 110.

9. The story of how he subsequently proceeded from a one-man show to the command of an empire is a fascinating tale (begin with Rockwell, *Rickover Effect*, and the two Duncan books, *Rickover and the Nuclear Navy* and *Rickover: The Struggle for Excellence*). In fact, the power struggle within the Navy bureaucracies and other government agencies is so remarkable it tends to distract from the much more fundamental question of what new and innovative management and leadership techniques Rickover introduced. I have deliberately chosen to ignore the rich tapestry of the distracting power struggle going on behind the Washington insiders' curtain.

10. From Rickover's 1954 speech to the Naval Postgraduate School:

"Some of the ideas I try to get across to the people who work for me are the following:

1. **More than ambition, more than ability, it is rules that limit contribution;** rules are the lowest common denominator of human behavior. They are a substitute for rational thought.

2. **Sit down before fact with an open mind.** Be prepared to give up every preconceived notion. Follow humbly wherever and to whatever abyss Nature leads or you learn nothing. Don't push out figures when facts are going in the opposite direction.

3. **Free discussion requires an atmosphere unembarrassed by any suggestion of authority or even respect.** If a subordinate always agrees with his superior he is a useless part of the organization. In this connection there is a story of Admiral Sims when he was on duty in London in World War I. He called a conscientious hard-working officer in to him to explain why he was dissatisfied with the officer's work. The officer blushed and stammered when Sims pointed out that in all the time they had been working together the officer had never once disagreed with Sims.

4. **All men are by nature conservative but conservatism in the military profession is a source of danger to the country.** One must be ready to change his line sharply and suddenly, with no concern for the prejudices and memories of what was yesterday. To rest upon formula is a slumber that, prolonged, means death.

5. **Success teaches us nothing; only failure teaches.**

6. **Do not regard loyalty as a personal matter.** A greater loyalty is one to the Navy or to the Country. When you know you are absolutely right, and when you are unable to do anything about it, complete military subordination to rules becomes a form of cowardice.

7. **To doubt one's own first principles is the mark of a civilized man.** Don't defend past actions; what is right today may be wrong tomorrow. Don't be consistent; consistency is the refuge of fools.

8. **Thoughts arising from *practical* experience may be a bridle or a spur.**

9. **Optimism and stupidity are nearly synonymous.**

10. **Avoid over-coordination.** We have all observed months-long delays caused by an effort to bring all activities into complete agreement with a proposed policy or procedure. While the coordinating machinery is slowly grinding away, the original purpose is often lost. The essence of the proposals is being worn down as the persons most concerned impatiently await the decision. **The process has been aptly called** *coordinating to death.*

11. **A system under which it takes three men to check what one is doing is not control; it is systematic strangulation.**

12. A man, by working 24 hours a day, could multiply himself 3 times. To multiply him more than 3 times the only recourse is to train others to take over some of his work."

11. His system had other subtle values. Those who brought up fraudulent challenges (i.e., their challenges were technically incorrect) to the system identified themselves as fools who needed more careful watching. At the same time, multiple challenges to the same processes, even if the challenges were flawed, indicated one of two issues. Either there was a misunderstanding of what the process was attempting to achieve, or there was a process flaw as yet uncovered. In any case, it indicated that a more flexible mind should reexamine the problem.

12. See, for example, Blair, *Atomic Submarine*, 23; and Hewlett and Duncan, *Nuclear Navy*, 24–48.

13. No edifice is ever built without a cultural change. I began my Navy life in diesel submarines (USS *Trumpetfish*), and I commanded the last squadron of diesel submarines in the American fleet. Just like the fabled skippers of World War II, I have drunk in the Clean Sweep Bar in Pearl Harbor and danced outside on the tiled floor under the palms and stars with my true love the evening before deploying for dangerous waters. In addition, that same woman and I built a room reserved for Medal of Honor winners and four-star admirals at the Submarine Sanctuary in Yokosuka, Japan, and there hosted Adm. Gene Fluckey, the World War II commanding officer who had been recognized with a Medal of Honor for his legendary patrols on board the diesel submarine USS *Barb* (SS-220), and his wife. I loved this culture that had to die.

14. This decision was contentious as critics maintain that one needs officers who are bold in battle. Rickover believed that since a submarine was a stealth weapon and often did its best work as a deterrent, having the ability to reliably start up the reactor plant and move a submarine under way and submerged (an act purely the product of a working engineering plant) not only provided deterrence but also was 80 percent of any other mission the submarine might assume. In addition, many senior submariners observed that, given the talent Rickover recruited, learning and demonstrating a command of tactics and warfighting were skills most nuclear-trained officers easily developed. I do not believe the argument was ever settled to the satisfaction of the critics. The secrecy of the most important submarine operations was a factor in keeping the discussion alive.

15. The stem is the thin round piece of steel projecting from the valve body that connects the operating handle to the mechanism interrupting the flow of water or steam.

16. The lubrication was designed to keep the graphite packing around the stem moist so that the valve could be operated (rotated) without excessive torque— but a nuclear submarine closes its hatches and stays submerged for months at a time, so the small leakage past the valve stems thoughtlessly added to the air-conditioning burden and slowly built up radioactivity (the tortuous trip by the rings of packing contained most of the radioactive particulate).

17. The argument over stopping of the release of radioactivity into the environment is only one of many conflicts Rickover had with the engineers in the Bureau of Ships (especially the admirals therein). In general, the admirals were not supportive of Rickover's approaches to nuclear design issues, nor were they much interested in submarines.

    Probably the nexus of Rickover's almost visceral negative reaction to the word manager was the perceived tendency of the Bureau of Ships at this time to be more interested in "managing" than in doing. In fact, the relationship between the nuclear and nonnuclear segments of the bureau was typically bitter for many years—and that emotional reaction was reflected throughout the fleet.

18. The leaking-valve issue (the bureau's reactor-support valves were designed to leak reactor coolant) was only one of many arguments. Rickover won this particular argument by defining the problem as one involving issues over which he had responsibility (reactor safety) and blandly declaring that no one could discharge radioactivity overboard. As a result, each commanding officer clamored for the valves originally placed in their submarine by the Bureau of Ships to be removed and replaced. Otherwise, to comply with Admiral Rickover's dictum, each ship had to construct elaborate plastic catch basins around each valve, filled with the equivalent of very absorbent paper towels.

19. We quickly learned that radioactive fluids could be gathered, contained, combined with other compounds to stabilize the mixture, and then shipped to controlled sites for burial.

20. For simply one example, see a conversation in 1947 between Captain Rickover and Ray Dick, a metallurgical engineer from Ohio State who was with Rickover in Oak Ridge and afterward, about approving the building of a nuclear submarine (Rockwell, *Rickover Effect*, 56):

    "Do we have any leads through his [the Secretary of the Navy] or any other staff types that could get us an audience?" asked Dick.

    "Naw, that's not going to do it. It's got to be somebody who can speak authoritatively on ships, on what kind of ships a fighting Navy needs." (Rickover)

    "That's what the Bureau of Ships is supposed to tell him." (Dick)

    "Oh, hell. No line officer thinks the bureau knows what it needs. When was the last time you heard a seagoing line officer listening with rapt attention to some character from BuShips?" (Rickover)

    "The only real authority on the needs of the fleet is the chief of naval operations, Captain. The rest of the guys are just an amen chorus." (Rickover)

21. Rickover kept extraordinary people in the nuclear-submarine force with leadership. While nuclear-trained people received bonuses as well as extra pay for being in submarines, the civilian commercial market was offering submariners

salaries double or triple the total Navy stipend. One of Rickover's key management methods was to publicly recognize his subordinates' talents. As an observer said at the time, "In his treatment of his men Rickover draws no lines of rank. The lowest of his subordinates can and does argue heatedly with him. Rickover delegates large amounts of responsibility and authority to his subordinates, thus giving them the satisfaction of conceiving *and* implementing ideas. This is rare in the Navy or in private industry, where brainworkers' children are customarily ripped untimely from them by the administrators. It is, indeed, the only coin sufficient to pay Rickover's men." (Wallace, "Deluge of Honors," 116.)

22. For example, the self-scuttling of the Yankee-class (K-219) submarine off Bermuda on 6 October 1986 after a fire in a missile tube.

23. As substantiation, let me provide you two examples of well-known failures caused by "heroes" drawn from the same American melting pot that provides submarine officer candidates. Culture failures overrode talent in the two National Aeronautics and Space Administration (NASA) flight disasters (1986 and 2003) and in the U.S. Air Force in 2008, when the service lost control of its nuclear weapons and the secretary of defense consequently fired its top political appointee and senior general.

Chapter 17. A Culture of Adaptation

1. Rickover, speech delivered to Naval Postgraduate School.

2. The last of the fleet boats, the B-girls (*Barbel*, *Blueback*, and *Bonefish*), were retired in 1990, 1990, and 1988, respectively, but the experimental submarine USS *Dolphin* (AGSS-555) was not decommissioned until 2007. This is not to say that the idea of diesel submarines has ever died for the United States, as whenever shipyards lobby for work or politicians look for increased hometown employment, diesel-like proposals inevitably rise.

3. And the surface ship–submarine capability gap was increasing. Under Rickover's system of process control, nuclear-submarine material standards had continuously ratcheted upward every year, significantly outpacing the standards accepted elsewhere.

4. Women pilots were landing on carriers in the Navy's high-performance airplanes. Many curmudgeons believed that women had no place in the Navy. This was especially evident within the retired ranks but also existed among active-duty personnel (surreptitiously aided and abetted by several key elected representatives in Congress). Change in the rest of the Navy had become inevitable after women had been accessed to seagoing positions while Admiral Zumwalt was Chief of Naval Operations. But by law there continued to be no females serving on board submarines.

5. I am avoiding discussing the nuclear-trained officers assigned to surface ships, as after we had been trained together, I did not subsequently serve nor mature with this group. As a consequence, I did not know this community nearly as well as I did the submarine officers.

6. After two decades of annual selection boards called to correct this "error," one begins to assume there is a powerful cultural reason this oversight has not been addressed by these closed-to-outsiders promotion boards.

7. No, his former staff at Naval Reactors was not thrilled. This is not a fairy tale in which everyone is always happy. In fact, my briefing to the Naval Reactors staff that day in that small hot room was an unpleasant occasion. However, I believe I have as much insight as anyone into how Rickover would have viewed this change. The decision was consistent with the culture he had taught us—I chose to believe he would have been pleased.

8. Or so reported by Sontag and Drew, *Blind Man's Bluff.*

9. A submarine is complicated to build, and the required skills are perishable. Several studies showed that it was important to keep the shipyard technical skills refreshed for the future when America again needed a large submarine force to control a "peer competitor."

10. The Navy's submarine component was labeled OP-02 in those days. The senior billet at this key juncture was held by the imaginative Vice Adm. Dan Cooper.

11. Dan Cooper had commissioned me to conduct this study, and I had done so, in secret, with five of the submarine force's brightest commanding officers, all of whom would later be promoted to admiral, as well as a brilliant senior analyst civilian from the Center for Naval Analysis.

12. Demonstrating his unusual acumen and breadth, a decade later the Honorable Dan Cooper served President G. W. Bush as the undersecretary for benefits in the Department of Veterans Affairs.

13. "In 1953 Rickover told BuPers [the Bureau of Personnel] that he wanted another woman officer, and they sent over Rebecca A. Lloyd, a recreation major from North Carolina with a master's degree in education (personnel administration) from New York University. Rickover hired her and, to her amazement, told her that she was going to be one of the eggheads. He asked if she had taken chemistry, and she said no, but she had taken a physics course once. He assigned her a self-study program in chemistry and told her he was putting her in charge of secondary system chemistry and heat exchangers. He told her new boss, Jim Cochran, that he'd better not see her at a typewriter.

   "Most of us figured he had probably done this to humiliate Cochran because he was presumably unhappy with how chemistry was being handled. But Becky Lloyd said that she took Rickover at this word; he just wanted to get a woman into the technical work, and thought she could do it. 'He seemed to be impressed with the fact that I had worked my way through college, including the master's degree, without any help from anyone,' she said recently. 'He valued hard work and motivation a lot more than credentials. That experience really changed my life. I learned that I could do things I would never even have considered trying before.' Nearly twenty years passed before women began graduating in significant numbers from engineering schools." (Rockwell, *Rickover Effect*, 84.)

   Ms. Lloyd went on to success in the business world, as noted in Gilliam, "UNCG to Award," which announced that she was receiving an honorary degree for helping fund the honors college: "Rebecca A. Lloyd, a Greensboro native who now lives in San Diego. A 1950 graduate of Woman's College (now UNCG); Lloyd spent 22 years in the U.S. Navy. Her service included four years working at the Naval Reactors Branch, the project that was headed by Adm.

Hyman Rickover and ultimately produced the nuclear navy. . . . From 1972 to 1999, she was president of her own real estate firm, Rebecca Lloyd Inc. . . . Her $4 million gift to UNCG in 2006 is providing an endowment to fund the Lloyd International Honors College, named in honor of her parents, Aubrey P. and Georgia Garrison Lloyd."

14. Jennie became one of the first two women to qualify in submarines, receiving her gold dolphins on 5 December 2012 in Kitsap-Bangor, Washington, as a member of the USS *Maine* (SSBN-741) Blue Crew. (Friedrich, "Navy Pins 1st.")

Afterword: Memorial Day

1. Rickover, "Thoughts on Man's Purpose."
2. As mentioned previously, the Soviets were able to read our submarine correspondence as a result of the Walker-Whitworth spy ring, which had sold submarine communication code lists to the Soviet Union. This quotation was provided to me by Vice Adm. J. D. Williams, who also gave me a copy of the chart and who was present that day in his role as commander, Sixth Fleet.
3. Kennan, "Sources of Soviet Conduct." This theory famously argued that "the main element of any United States policy toward the Soviet Union must be that of long-term, patient but firm and vigilant containment of Russian expansive tendencies. . . . Russia will remain economically a vulnerable, and in a certain sense an impotent, nation, capable of exporting its enthusiasms and of radiating the strange charm of its primitive political vitality but unable to back up those articles of export by the real evidences of material power and prosperity. . . . But the possibility remains (and in the opinion of this writer it is a strong one) that Soviet power, like the capitalist world of its conception, bears within it the seeds of its own decay, and that the sprouting of these seeds is well advanced."

Bibliography

Allen, Thomas B., and Norman Polmar. *Rickover: Father of the Nuclear Navy*. Washington, DC: Potomac Books, 2007.

Anderson, William R. *The Ice Diaries: The Untold Story of the USS* Nautilus *and the Cold War's Most Daring Mission*. With Don Keith. Nashville, TN: Thomas Nelson, 2007.

Backus, Paul H. *The Reminiscences of Commander Paul H. Backus, U.S. Navy (Ret.)*. Interviewed by Paul Stillwell. Annapolis, MD: U.S. Naval Institute, 1995.

Bagley, Worth. *The Reminiscences of Staff Officers of Admiral Elmo R. Zumwalt Jr., U.S. Navy*. Interviewed by Paul Stillwell. Annapolis, MD: U.S. Naval Institute, 1988.

Barlow, Jeffery G. *Revolt of the Admirals: The Fight for Naval Aviation, 1945–1950*. Washington, DC: Naval Historical Center, 1994.

Bauer, Hermann. *Das Unterseeboot* [The Submarine: Its Importance as Part of a Fleet, Its Position in International Law, Its Employment in War, Its Future]. Translated by H. G. Rickover. Newport, RI: Department of Intelligence, Naval War College, July 1936.

Benson, Roy S. *The Reminiscences of Rear Admiral Roy S. Benson, U.S. Navy (Ret.)*. Vol. 1. Interviewed by Paul Stillwell. Annapolis, MD: U.S. Naval Institute, 1984.

Bentley, John. *The* Thresher *Disaster: The Most Tragic Dive in Submarine History*. New York: Doubleday, 1975.

Berham, Larry. *Zumwalt: The Life and Times of Admiral Elmo Russell "Bud" Zumwalt, Jr.* New York: Harper, 2012.

Beshany, Philip A. *The Reminiscences of Vice Admiral Philip A. Beshany, U.S. Navy (Ret.)*. 2 vols. Interviewed by John T. Mason Jr. Annapolis, MD: U.S. Naval Institute, 1980.

Bilby, Joseph G. *A Revolution in Arms: A History of the First Repeating Rifles*. Yardley, PA: Westholme, 2005.

Blair, Clay, Jr. *The Atomic Submarine and Admiral Rickover.* New York: Harry Holt, 1954.

———. "Atomic Submarines: In Sea Power, Another Revolution: The Man in Tempo 3." *Time,* 11 January 1954, 36–39.

Burke, Julian T., Jr. *The Reminiscences of Rear Admiral Julian T. Burke Jr., U.S. Navy (Ret.).* Interviewed by Paul Stillwell. Annapolis, MD: U.S. Naval Institute, 2003.

Cantonwine, Paul E., comp. *The Never-Ending Challenge of Engineering: Admiral H. G. Rickover in His Own Words.* La Grange Park, IL: American Nuclear Society, 2013.

Colbus, Louis. *The Reminiscences of Captain Louis Colbus, U.S. Navy (Ret.).* Interviewed by Paul Stillwell. Annapolis, MD: U.S. Naval Institute, 2001.

Cutter, Slade. *The Reminiscences of Captain Slade D. Cutter, U.S. Navy (Ret.).* 2 vols. Interviewed by Paul Stillwell. Annapolis, MD: U.S. Naval Institute, 1985.

Duncan, Charles K. *The Reminiscences of Admiral Charles K. Duncan, U.S. Navy (Ret.).* 4 vols. Interviewed by John T. Mason Jr. Annapolis, MD: U.S. Naval Institute, 1978.

Duncan, Francis. *Rickover and the Nuclear Navy: The Discipline of Technology.* Annapolis, MD: U.S. Naval Institute, 1990.

———. *Rickover: The Struggle for Excellence.* Annapolis, MD: U.S. Naval Institute, 2001.

Dunford, James Marshall. *Memoirs.* 1994. Personal family correspondence held by Louise Dunford Brodnitz.

Flynn, Jackie. "Navy Penalizes GD for Misconduct." *The Day* (New London, CT), 22 May 1985.

Friedman, Norman. *U.S. Submarines since 1945.* Annapolis, MD: U.S. Naval Institute, 1994.

Friedrich, Ed. "Navy Pins 1st Nuclear-Qualified Female Submariners." *Kitsap Sun,* 6 December 2012.

Gilliam, Steve. "UNCG to Award Two Honorary Degrees at May 16 Commencement." *High Point University News* (Greensboro, NC), June 2012.

Hewlett, Richard G., and Francis Duncan. *Nuclear Navy: 1946–1962.* Chicago: University of Chicago Press, 1974.

James, Ralph K. *The Reminiscences of Rear Admiral Ralph K. James, U.S. Navy (Ret.).* Interviewed by John T. Mason Jr. Annapolis, MD: U.S. Naval Institute, 1972.

Johnston, Wm. Robert, comp. "Deadliest Radiation Accidents and Other Events Causing Radiation Casualties." *Database of Radiological Incidents and Related Events—Johnston's Archive,* 23 September 2007. http://www.john stonsarchive.net/nuclear/radevents/radevents1.html.

Kelso, Frank. *The Reminiscences of Admiral Frank Kelso, U.S. Navy (Ret.).* Interviewed by Paul Stillwell. Annapolis, MD: U.S. Naval Institute, 2009.

Kennan, George F. [X, pseud.] "The Sources of Soviet Conduct." *Foreign Affairs* 25 (July 1947): 566–82.

Kennedy, Joel. "Another Theory on Loss of the USS *Scorpion.*" *The Stupid Shall Be Punished* (blog). 18 August 2010. http://bubbleheads.blogspot.com/2010/08 /another-theory-on-loss-of-uss-scorpion.html.

Kerr, Alex A. *The Reminiscences of Captain Alex A. Kerr, U.S. Navy (Ret.)*. Interviewed by Paul Stillwell. Annapolis, MD: U.S. Naval Institute, 1984.

Kotter, John. "What Leaders Really Do." *Harvard Business Review* 68, no. 3 (1 May 1990): 103–11.

Kuhn, Thomas. *The Structure of Scientific Revolution*. Chicago: University of Chicago Press, 1962.

Lake, Simon. *Submarine: The Autobiography of Simon Lake as Told to Herbert Corey*. New York: D. Appleton-Century, 1938.

Lecaque, Thomas. "The Guns That Almost Won the West: Repeating Weapons and the American Western Frontier." Monograph, Truman State University, Kirksville, MO, 2006.

Lee, Bill. "The Admiral and Me . . . And the Bullring." Newport News Apprentice Alumni Association, March 2006. http://www.nnapprentice.com/alumni/letter /THE_Admiral_and_Me.pdf.

Lee, Kent L. *The Reminiscences of Vice Admiral Kent L. Lee, U.S. Navy (Ret.)*. 2 vols. Interviewed by Paul Stillwell. Annapolis, MD: U.S. Naval Institute, 1990.

Libby, Ruthven E. *The Reminiscences of Vice Admiral Ruthven E. Libby, U.S. Navy (Ret.)*. Interviewed by Etta-Belle Kitchen. Annapolis, MD: U.S. Naval Institute, 1984.

Long, Robert L. J. *The Reminiscences of Admiral Robert L. J. Long, U.S. Navy (Ret.)*. Interviewed by Paul Stillwell. Annapolis, MD: U.S. Naval Institute, 1995.

Loughlin, Charles E. *The Reminiscences of Rear Admiral Charles E. Loughlin, U.S. Navy (Ret.)*. Interviewed by John T. Mason Jr. Annapolis, MD: U.S. Naval Institute, 1982.

Lyon, Waldo K. *The Reminiscences of Waldo K. Lyon, PhD, Director, Arctic Submarine Laboratory*. Interviewed by Etta-Belle Kitchen. Annapolis, MD: U.S. Naval Institute, 1971.

Mack, William P. *The Reminiscences of Vice Admiral William P. Mack, U.S. Navy (Ret.)*. 2 vols. Interviewed by John T. Mason Jr. Annapolis, MD: U.S. Naval Institute, 1980.

McNitt, Robert W. *The Reminiscences of Rear Admiral Robert W. McNitt, U.S. Navy (Ret.)*. Interviewed by Paul Stillwell. Annapolis, MD: U.S. Naval Institute, 2002.

Moorer, Thomas H. *The Reminiscences of Admiral Thomas H. Moorer, U.S. Navy (Ret.)*. 3 vols. Interviewed by John T. Mason Jr. Annapolis, MD: U.S. Naval Institute, 1981.

Morrison, Elting. *Men, Machines and Modern Times*. Boston: MIT Press, 1968.

Mumma, Albert G. *The Reminiscences of Rear Admiral Albert G. Mumma, U.S. Navy (Ret.)*. Interviewed by Paul Stillwell. Annapolis, MD: U.S. Naval Institute, 2001.

Nilsen, Thomas, Igor Kudrik, and Alexandr Nitkin. "The Russian Northern Fleet Nuclear Submarine Accidents." *Bellona Report*, no. 2:96 (5 October 1997). http://spb.org.ru/bellona/ehome/russia/nfl/nfl8.htm#O17.

Nixon, Richard. "Remarks at a Promotion Ceremony for Admiral Hyman G. Rickover," 3 December 1973. In *The American Presidency Project*, ed. Gerhard Peters and John T. Woolley. http://www.presidency.ucsb.edu /ws/?pid=4058.

Offley, Ed. *Scorpion Down: Sunk by the Soviets, Buried by the Pentagon: The Untold Story.* New York: Perseus Books, 2007.

Oliver, David R., Jr. "Secretary McNamara, The Navy and the CVA-67 Controversy." Master's diss., American University, June 1974.

Peet, Raymond E. *The Reminiscences of Vice Admiral Raymond E. Peet, U.S. Navy (Ret.).* Interviewed by Etta-Belle Kitchen. Annapolis, MD: U.S. Naval Institute, 1984.

Polmar, Norman. "Re: 'Loss of USS *Scorpion.*'" *Submarine Review,* Summer 2012, 141.

Polmar, Norman, and Thomas B. Allen. *Rickover: Controversy and Genius.* New York: Simon & Schuster, 1982.

Ramage, Lawson Paterson. *The Reminiscences of Vice Admiral Lawson Paterson Ramage, U.S. Navy (Ret.).* Interviewed by John T. Mason Jr. Annapolis, MD: U.S. Naval Institute, 1974.

Reich, Eli T. *The Reminiscences of Vice Admiral Eli T. Reich, U.S. Navy (Ret.).* 2 vols. Interviewed by John T. Mason Jr. Annapolis, MD: U.S. Naval Institute, 1979.

Rickover, Hyman G. *American Education, a National Failure: The Problem of Our Schools and What We Can Learn from England.* New York: E. P. Dutton, 1963.

———. "Doing a Job." Speech delivered at Columbia University School of Engineering, New York, 5 November 1982.

———. *Education and Freedom.* New York: E. P. Dutton, 1959.

———. "Getting the Job Done Right." *New York Times,* 25 November 1981.

———. Interview by Diane Sawyer. *60 Minutes,* CBS, 1984. Accessed 5 February 2012. http://www.people.vcu.edu/~rsleeth/Rickover.html.

———. Speech delivered to Naval Postgraduate School, Monterey, CA, 16 March 1954. In Cantonwine, *Never-Ending Challenge of Engineering,* chap. 10.

———. *Swiss Schools and Ours: Why Theirs Are Better.* Boston: Little, Brown: 1962.

———. "Thoughts on Man's Purpose in Life." Speech delivered at San Diego Rotary Club, San Diego, CA, 10 February 1977.

———. "The World of the Uneducated." *Saturday Evening Post,* 28 November 1959, 19, 54–59.

Rickover, Ruth Masters. *Pepper, Rice, and Elephants: A Southeast Asian Journey from Celebes to Siam.* Annapolis, MD: U.S. Naval Institute, 1975.

Riddell, Richard A. *Through My Periscope: A Recollection of my Life.* Arlington, VA: Sheridan Books, 2013.

Rivero, Horatio, Jr. *The Reminiscences of Admiral Horatio Rivero Jr., U.S. Navy (Ret.).* Interviewed by John T. Mason Jr. Annapolis, MD: U.S. Naval Institute, 1978.

Rockwell, Theodore. *Creating the New World: Stories and Images from the Dawn of the Atomic Age.* Bloomington, IN: 1st Books Library, 2003.

———. *The Rickover Effect: How One Man Made a Difference.* Annapolis, MD: U.S. Naval Institute, 1992. Reprint, Lincoln, NE: iUniverse, 2002.

Romig, Mary F. *Fatal Submarine Accidents: A Bibliography, 1900–1965.* Santa Monica, CA: Rand, November 1966.

Russell, James S. *The Reminiscences of Rear Admiral James S. Russell, U.S. Navy (Ret.)*. Interviewed by John T. Mason Jr. Annapolis, MD: U.S. Naval Institute, 1976.

Sagerholm, James. "The Great Draft of 1963." *Submarine Review*, 12 January 2011, 25–28.

Schratz, Paul R. "Admiral Rickover and the Cult of Personality." *Air University Review* 34, no. 5 (July/August 1983): 96–101.

Schumacher, Mary. *Trident: Setting the Requirements*. Case Program C-15-88-802.0. Cambridge, MA: Kennedy School of Government, 1987.

Shear, Harold E. *The Reminiscences of Admiral Harold E. Shear, U.S. Navy (Ret.)*. Interviewed by Paul Stillwell. Annapolis, MD: U.S. Naval Institute, 1997.

Smedberg, William R., III. *The Reminiscences of Vice Admiral William R. Smedberg III, U.S. Navy (Ret.)*. 2 vols. Interviewed by John T. Mason Jr. Annapolis, MD: U.S. Naval Institute, 1979.

Sontag, Sherry, and Christopher Drew. *Blind Man's Bluff: The Untold Story of American Submarine Espionage*. New York: Public Affairs, 1998.

Summitt, Dan. *Tales of a Cold War Submariner*. College Station: Texas A&M University Press, 2004.

Time. "We Will Bury You." Foreign News, 26 November 1956.

Train, Harry D., II. *The Reminiscences of Admiral Harry D. Train II, U.S. Navy (Ret.)*. Interviewed by Paul Stillwell. Annapolis, MD: U.S. Naval Institute, 1997.

Turner, Stansfield. *The Reminiscences of Admiral Stansfield Turner, U.S. Navy (Ret.)*. Interviewed by John T. Mason Jr. Annapolis, MD: U.S. Naval Institute, 2011.

Tyler, Patrick. *Running Critical: The Silent War, Rickover and General Dynamics*. New York: Harper & Row, 1986.

Valor at Sea. "U.S. Submarine Losses in World War II." 2002. http://www.valoratsea.com/losses1.htm.

Wallace, Robert. "A Deluge of Honors for an Exasperating Admiral." *Life*, 8 September 1958, 104–18.

Ward, Norvell G. *The Reminiscences of Rear Admiral Norvell G. Ward, U.S. Navy (Ret.)*. Interviewed by Paul Stillwell. Annapolis, MD: U.S. Naval Institute, 1996.

Wertheim, Robert H. *The Reminiscences of Rear Admiral Robert H. Wertheim, U.S. Navy (Ret.)*. Interviewed by John T. Mason Jr. Annapolis, MD: U.S. Naval Institute, 1979.

Wilkinson, Eugene P. "Abandoning the *Darter*." In *Submarine Stories: Recollections from the Diesel Boats*, edited by Paul Stillwell, 185. Annapolis, MD: Naval Institute Press, 2007.

———. *The Reminiscences of Vice Admiral Eugene P. Wilkinson, U.S. Navy (Ret.)*. Interviewed by Paul Stillwell. Annapolis, MD: U.S. Naval Institute, 2006.

Williams, Joe, Jr. *The Reminiscences of Vice Admiral Joe Williams Jr., U.S. Navy (Ret.)*. Interviewed by Paul Stillwell. Annapolis, MD: U.S. Naval Institute, 2002.

World Nuclear Association. "Nuclear-Powered Ships." March 2014. http://world-nuclear.org/info/Non-Power-Nuclear-Applications/Transport/Nuclear-Powered-Ships

Zumwalt, Elmo R., Jr. *On Watch*. Arlington, VA: Admiral Zumwalt and Associates, 1976.

Index

accidents. *See* nuclear reactor
  accidents; safety issues
accountability: of leader, 95–99;
  in reactor reinspection, 57–58;
  Rickover on, 31, 38–39, 57–58
active sonar, 41
Airbus, 153n17
aircraft carrier maintenance, 155n5
aircraft carriers, 129–30, 131, 157n3
Akhromeyev, Sergei F., 137
Allyn Mountain, 100
Alonzo Stagg Field, 15
American Medical Building
  Corporation, 83
Ames, Aldrich, 110
Anderson, Bill, 24, 28, 29, 30, 141n5,
  142n3
antiwar movement, 87
Argonne National Laboratory, 17
arms race, 142n5
asymmetric warfare, 9, 29, 142n5
Atomic Energy Commission, 16, 19,
  122
Atomic Submarine (Blair), 140n2
at risk advantage, 110, 156n5
attack submarine, 103, 110, 128, 131,
  154n2
Aurand, Evan Peter "Pete," 26, 28, 30,
  142n6
automotive industry, 147n4

"balance of terror," 21
ballistic-missile submarine, 33, 96,
  109, 150n3
Barb (SS-220), 160n13
battery charging: diesel versus nuclear
  submarine, 42–43; Operation
  Baker process, 43–45
battery explosion, 43, 145n6
Bay of Pigs invasion, 135
Beach, Ingrid, 142n7
Beach, Ned, 29, 142n7
Bednowicz, Eleonore A., 4
Berlin airlift, 135
Berlin Blockade, 8
Beshany, Phil, 151n2
best practices, 73
Bethesda Naval Hospital, 55
B-girls submarines, 162n2
Bremerton naval base, 155n6. *See also*
  Puget Sound Naval Shipyard
Bureau of Personnel, 63
Bureau of Ships, 4, 143n3; nuclear and
  nonnuclear division animosity in,
  161n17; safety issues and, 32
Bureau of Ships manual, 144n4
Bush, George H.W., 137

Calvert, Jim, 143n8
Cavite Navy Yard, 4
Chief of Naval Operations, 91,
  153n13, 153n15

About the Author

Dave Oliver's diverse career has included extensive experience in government and industry as well as the military.

He served the Clinton administration as principal deputy undersecretary of defense for acquisition, technology, and logistics and the Bush administration in Iraq as the director of management and budget for the coalition forces.

In industry Dave was the CEO of the EADS, North America Defense Company as well as chief operating officer of the main American organization. He was an executive at Northrop Grumman and at Westinghouse.

Dave spent thirty-two years in the Navy, retiring as a rear admiral (upper half). He served at sea on board both diesel-electric and nuclear submarines, commanded a nuclear submarine as well as the submarine groups in Japan and a second in San Diego; and served as Chief of Staff of the Seventh Fleet. His final military tour was as principal deputy to the civilian Navy acquisition executive.

Dave's military decorations include the Defense and Navy Distinguished Service Medals as well as six awards of the Legion of Merit. His awards for public service include two Department of Defense awards for Distinguished Public Service and similar awards from the Departments of the Army and the Navy.

Dave's undergraduate training was from the United States Naval Academy. He subsequently received a Master of Arts in political science and international affairs (specializing in the Middle East) from American University. He is also the author of *Making It in Washington,* which deals with serving as a political appointee, as well as his wife's biography, *Wide Blue Ribbon,* and an earlier leadership book, *Lead On.*